Catherine de' Medici and the Protestant Reformation

Catherine de' Medici and the Protestant Reformation

Nancy Whitelaw

MORGAN
REYNOLDS
Publishing, Inc.

620 South Elm Street, Suite 223
Greensboro, North Carolina 27406
http://www.morganreynolds.com

European Queens

Queen Isabella
Catherine de' Medici
Catherine the Great
Marie Antoinette
Queen Victoria

CATHERINE DE' MEDICI AND THE PROTESTANT REFORMATION

Copyright © 2005 by Nancy Whitelaw

Library of Congress Cataloging-in-Publication Data

Whitelaw, Nancy.
Catherine de' Medici and the Protestant Reformation / Nancy Whitelaw.—
1st ed.
p. cm. — (European queens)
Includes bibliographical references and index.
ISBN 1-931798-26-5 (library binding)
1. Catherine de Médicis, Queen, consort of Henry II, King of France,
1519-1589—Juvenile literature. 2. Queens—France—Biography—Juvenile
literature. 3. France—Church history—16th century—Juvenile literature.
4. Reformation—France—Juvenile literature. I. Title. II. Series.
DC119.8.W45 2004
944'.028—dc22

2004014716

Printed in the United States of America
First Edition

Dedicated with love to Donna Burgio Gosciak,
a woman of remarkable strength and courage

Contents

1

Born into Chaos

The wedding of fourteen-year-old Caterina Maria Romola de' Medici to Henry, Duke of Orléans, second in line to the French throne, was one of the most splendid events of the sixteenth century. It took months to plan the ceremony that brought guests from all over Europe to the French harbor city of Marseilles. There were hundreds of rules of etiquette and diplomatic protocols which had to be followed; it was imperative the wedding go off without a hitch. After all, this wedding, like most royal ones, was not about celebrating the love between the bride and bridegroom (the two had not yet even met) but about cementing political alliances in Europe. Fourteen-year-old Caterina, an orphan, was given in marriage by her great-uncle, Pope Clement VII, in a gamble he hoped would safeguard the Medici family and shore up the

Opposite: Catherine de' Medici

Caterina at the time of her marriage.

boundaries of his Italian states.

France and Spain, two of the most powerful countries of the day, had long been at war over the city-states of Italy. Each wanted more territory, people, and power. During the 1500s, Italy was not a unified country but rather a collection of rival city-states. By 1516, Spain controlled most of southern Italy (including Sicily and Naples) while France controlled most of northern Italy (Milan). The Papal States, under the control of the pope and the Medici family, were stuck right in the middle.

The Medici family, one of the wealthiest in Europe, was generally unpopular. Their rise to power began in the fourteenth century when they parlayed control of the largest banks in several European cities into the *de facto* rule of Florence. Becoming enormously wealthy through money lending is never a path to popularity, but the Medici had added to their notoriety by earning a reputation for power lust and evildoing. The use of poisons to eliminate political rivals was considered to be the Medici's weapon of choice. Many in France used the family name as a synonym for "poisoner." Young Caterina knew that the people of France considered her to be an ill-suited bride. Not only was her family regarded as devious and dangerous, they were not truly nobility. When Clement tried to marry her to the Duke of Orléans's older brother, the dauphin of France, he had been flatly rejected. Caterina's blood was not good enough for the heir to the French throne.

Francis I, the king of France, had only consented to match his younger son to a Medici because he hoped to yoke the strength of that family to his own in order to defeat the Spanish. Francis had married his cousin to another Medici and the couple became Caterina's parents, so he was not as resistant as the rest of France to welcoming her into his own family. Francis was not very close to his son Henry because the boy had been raised apart from his father for many years. For his part, Henry deeply resented being forced to marry a Medici, a woman he thought was beneath him, and he was extremely cold to his new bride.

Despite these tensions, the many nuptial ceremonies proceeded smoothly. The families exchanged gifts—a tapestry depicting the Last Supper for the pope and the tusk of an elephant mounted in gold for the king. Then, on October 28, 1533, Pope Clement presided at the wedding. The bride wore a gown of brocade trimmed with ermine and a crown so heavily laden with jewels she had to strain to hold her head steady as she walked down the aisle. More jewels were woven into her thick dark hair. Henry was dressed in elegant clothes also studded with jewels. After the ceremony, Francis kissed his new daughter-in-law, complimented her on her

The marriage of Catherine de' Medici to Henry, Duke of Orléans, as presided over by Pope Clement VII. *(Courtesy of Art Resource.)*

appearance, and called her daughter. When he asked to be allowed to use the French version of her name, Catherine, she smiled and agreed. Caterina Maria Romola de' Medici was now Catherine, Duchess of Orléans.

Having a title was new for the Medici family. Catherine's father, Lorenzo, had only been able to marry her mother after being granted a noble title—he was made the Duke of Urbino just months before their wedding in 1518. Two things became apparent soon after their nuptial ceremony: Madeline was pregnant and Lorenzo was dying. He had contracted tuberculosis.

Madeline delivered a daughter on April 13, 1519. But the joyous occasion soon turned tragic. The young mother contracted puerperal fever—the all-purpose name given to infections contracted during childbirth—and never left her bed. She died on April 28. Five days later Lorenzo was gone. The newborn inherited the title Duchess of Urbino and began her life as an orphan ensnared in the internecine world of European politics.

Catherine's parents had been married during a brief interlude in the wars between France and Spain. When Catherine was three, those wars resumed. She spent her early years in Rome, living under the protection of her great-uncle, Pope Leo X, and his cousin Cardinal Giulio de' Medici. When Pope Leo died, Adrian VI, who was not a

Pope Leo X, Catherine's guardian, with his cousin Cardinal Giulio, who would become Pope Clement VII, to his right. *(Uffizi Gallery, Florence.)*

Medici, was chosen by the college of cardinals to succeed him. Giulio had expected to be elected pope and made no effort to hide his displeasure at being passed over. He left Rome for a time. Soon after his return, Pope Adrian VI died. Inevitably, it was rumored he had been poisoned. It is possible the cardinals believed the rumors because they did not disappoint Giulio again. He became pope in November 1523 and took the name Clement VII.

Although he was the spiritual leader of the Catholic Church, Clement wanted, first and foremost, to restore his family to power. His second goal, which was closely intertwined with his first, was to devise a strategy to play the powerful French and Spanish forces against one another. He hoped they would exhaust each other and leave Italy, which had been the victim of both countries' imperial dreams for a generation.

Unfortunately, Clement's dreams outpaced his skills. In the Middle Ages it had been possible for a pope to use his authority as God's vicar to control the secular rulers of Europe. Then, the threat of excommunication, which condemned the offender to an eternity of hellfire, could bring even the most powerful ruler to his knees. But the political dynamics of Europe had changed. A process of secularization had begun with the Renaissance, and by the early sixteenth century, the fear of eternal damnation did not have the same terrorizing power over most European rulers.

Clement began his attempt at diplomacy by signing a treaty with Francis I of France. Then in 1525, at the Battle of Pavia (a city outside of Milan in northern Italy), Francis

Opposite: The Battle of Pavia.

suffered a terrible defeat. When Pope Clement heard the news, he tried to negotiate a treaty with the victor, king of Spain and Holy Roman Emperor Charles V, but it was too late. Charles realized Clement was trying to play both sides, and he was very angry. He forced the captive Francis to sign the Treaty of Madrid, according to which Francis gave up all of France's claims to Italy and surrendered the province of Burgundy to Spain. Most humiliating was Charles's insistence that the recently widowed Francis agree to marry his sister Eleanor. To make sure he followed through on the agreement, Francis had to hand over his two oldest sons as hostages, to be returned after the wedding.

After the king was released, and his sons were imprisoned in a dark castle in far away Madrid, Francis reneged on the agreement. He sent word to Charles that he would rather marry his mule than the emperor's sister and refused to cede any land or make any of the payments they had agreed upon. Charles was now furious with both Francis and Pope Clement for betraying him.

The army Charles had fielded against the French was made up largely of German mercenaries—many of whom were Protestant and therefore enemies of the Catholic Church. It was less than ten years since the former monk Martin Luther had defied the authority of the Catholic Church and began the Protestant Reformation—religious tensions were at a fever pitch. After the Spanish victory at Pavia, Charles's army was at loose ends. When word spread that the soldiers would not be paid for their duty because Charles was nearly broke, this group of highly trained killers began to move down the Italian peninsula toward Rome. Though Charles was Catholic, he made no effort to stop them—it's possible he was willing to see Pope Clement punished.

Two years after Pavia, in 1527, the hungry army entered the holy city and released their pent-up frustrations and religious anger in an explosion of violence. For eight days and nights the citizens of Rome suffered almost continuous horror. It is estimated that nearly fifteen thousand people, out of a population of fifty-five thousand, were murdered. Thousands more were raped, injured, and looted of their

Soldiers entering Rome during the sack of the city. *(Courtesy of Art Resource.)*

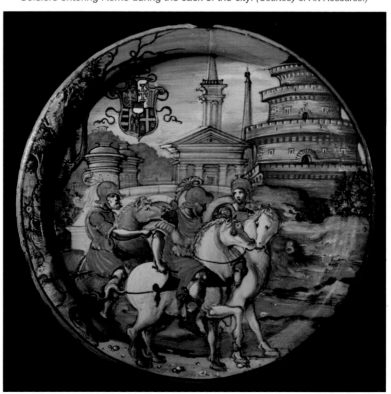

worldly possessions. The indignity was not only material. One mob of German mercenaries held a ceremony and proclaimed Martin Luther, the Protestant leader, the new pope. Another crowned a donkey as the Vicar of Christ and paid homage to him in a mock ceremony. One German leader wore around his neck a heavy chain that he claimed he would use to choke the pope to death if he caught him. But the pope managed to slip out of the city disguised as a servant.

Catherine had been sent away before the attack. She was too important to Pope Clement's future plans to risk losing. She had been placed in the care of an aunt who had taken her to Florence to be protected by Cardinal Silvio Passerini.

When word of the sack of Rome arrived in Florence, the citizens, who deeply hated Cardinal Passerini, seized the opportunity to revolt against Medici rule. On May 19, an assembly met in the Palazzo della Signoria and declared that Florence was once again a republic. They also promised to guarantee Catherine's safety. The assembly forbade her to leave the city—they wanted her as a hostage in case Pope Clement attacked. She was sent to the convent of Santa Lucia, where she stayed for the next six months, before being moved to the larger convent of the Santissima Annunziata delle Murate.

The sisters of the Murate came from Italy's most prominent families. Catherine was eight years old when she walked into the convent. She was moved because the plague was rampant in Florence and she would be safer in the more isolated convent located on the wealthier side of the city.

During Catherine's first eleven months at the Murate, Florence was besieged by many of the same mercenaries

This painting by Giorgio Vasari shows Catherine's hometown of Florence during the siege. *(Palazzo Vecchio, Florence)*

that had sacked Rome. This time the soldiers for hire were being paid by Pope Clement, who was determined to overthrow the newly declared republic.

As the battle between Clement's soldiers and the leaders of Florence raged, Catherine's life was in grave danger. She could have been seized by the republican leaders at any time. There was discussion of stripping her naked and strapping her to the walls of the city; or of forcing her into a brothel, which would destroy her value on the European royal marriage market.

On the night of July 19, 1530, the leaders of Florence's revolutionaries knocked on the convent gates and demanded that Catherine be turned over to them. The nuns were terrified but Catherine ordered them to deny the men entrance. As one nun remembered, Catherine "refused with wonderful firmness and resolution." When the men grew frustrated and left, Catherine went to her room, hacked off her hair, and dressed herself in the habit of a nun. "Will they dare now to remove me?" she asked. Catherine was counting on appearances to save herself: she believed the republicans would not risk the shame of appearing to kidnap a nun.

A month later, the Florentines surrendered to the pope's mercenaries, and Catherine was safe. For the rest of her life, Catherine looked back at her time at the Murate fondly. As an adult, she granted the order large gifts of money, jewels, and land as gratitude for their care and protection.

The sack of Rome and the subsequent battles in Florence made a deep impression on young Catherine. She would harbor a distrust of Germans for the rest of her life, and never forgot the kind of crimes people were capable of committing in the name of religion.

Those who met and wrote about Catherine as a girl were quick to remark on her intelligence, agile mind, and gracious manners. Despite the chaos that had enveloped her life, the nuns had done a good job of educating her. She enjoyed outside activities, especially horseback riding. Small boned and thin, her most noticeable feature was the large, dark, and slightly protruding eyes that were characteristic of the Medici.

While Rome and Florence had been attacked by the remnants of Charles's army, Francis's repudiation of the Treaty of Madrid had led to yet another war between the French and the Spanish. Francis lost again, and the Treaty of Cambrai (1529) established Spanish victory.

Catherine was returned to Rome in 1530, and six months later, negotiations began between Pope Clement and Francis to arrange her marriage to the Duke of Orléans. Pope Clement offered Francis a generous cash dowry. The French king was happy to accept both the money and the implied support of the powerful Medicis. After the agreement was finalized in 1531, Catherine was returned to the Murate in Florence.

The nuns were happy to have her back. Her education continued along with the preparations for her wedding. Meanwhile, the beleaguered citizens of Florence were taxed to pay for her dowry, as well as for the cost of transporting her entourage to Marseilles, and the jewels, gowns, horses, and various other expenses necessary to marry her off.

On September 1, 1533, Catherine, accompanied by her aunt, a cousin, and dozens of attendants, left her ancestral home of Florence for the last time. Her first fourteen years of life had been filled with death, grief, and political chaos. This would prove to be excellent preparation for what was to follow.

2

The Valois Court

Francis I had planned the wedding of Catherine and Henry to be the grandest in recent memory because he wanted everything he did to be bigger, more fabulous, and more expensive than what other sovereigns could muster. His grandiosity was partly due to his ego and larger-than-life personality, but there was also a more practical reason. Any ambitious noble who wanted to be king would have to think long and hard before challenging such an imposing figure, one who seemed to bring glory to France by his very existence.

France had become a more unified country over the last hundred years. The unification had begun in 1425, when Joan of Arc had led a reinvigorated French army against the occupying English. Gradually, the powerful nobles of France had been brought under the control of a single king, but the nobility remained wealthy and powerful. Francis had to remain in the good graces of his Royal Council of noble advisors. Occasionally, events required him to call a meeting of the Estates General, an assembly made up of leaders from the towns and villages, the landed nobility, and the leaders of the Catholic Church in France. French monarchs were not absolute rulers—they were answerable to their population and, more specifically, to their nobility in a way other European kings were not.

After Catherine's marriage, she and her new husband went to live at Francis's court. Just a few months later, Pope Clement died—rendering the agreement he had made with Francis useless. Although he did not gain anything from the marriage of Catherine and Henry, Francis did not take his frustration out on her. However, most of the French court did not hesitate to let their unfavorable opinion of the Medici bride be known. Catherine's marriage, as one observer reported, "dissatisfies the entire nation." Francis, though, had grown fond of the new Duchess of Orléans. He admired her intelligence and her quiet strength. Francis had inherited his determination and strong will from his mother— his father had died when he was an infant—and some thought Catherine reminded him of her. Catherine admired the king's self-confidence, as well as his enthusiastic appreciation of literature and art. To Catherine, her father-in-law was a ray of light, so unlike her petulant and self-pitying husband.

Francis wanted the women in his court to be knowledgeable and intelligent. Italy was a center of artistic genius, and much of the art of France had its roots in Italy. In Rome, Catherine had even seen the latest paintings by Sandro Botticelli and those of Michelangelo Buonarroti whose frescoes adorned the ceiling of the Sistine Chapel. She had lived amongst the Renaissance sculpture and architecture of Florence. Both Francis and Catherine were drawn to what was called the New Learning, a focus on philosophy that encouraged creative thinking. She had studied mathematics, poetry, and art, as well as Latin and Greek.

Catherine was also interested in geography, physics, and astronomy, topics usually reserved for men. She brought a belief in astrology from her mother country. In the sixteenth century this was a respectable science, and Catherine's scientific inclination led her to a deeper study of the stars. She owned a book with bronze pages on which rotating disks represented

Botticelli's "Primavera" or "Allegory of Spring" is renowned for its intricate symbolism and attention to the proportion and beauty of the human form. *(Uffizi Gallery, Florence)*

King Francis I. *(Louvre, Paris)*

the constellations. She could turn the disks to create the conjunctions necessary to read horoscopes. She believed that the stars influenced the health and lives of people, and kept notes on the predictions about her own life she gleaned from the study. She noted with satisfaction that in 1533, around the date of her marriage, a comet appeared—a promising sign.

Catherine found it easier to please King Francis than to please her new husband. Four years held hostage in Spain had formed Henry's personality. He found it difficult to share his thoughts. The father and son were deeply estranged. King Francis openly favored Henry's older brother, and Henry did not bother try to please his father or his other relatives and friends. One contemporary observed, "He laughs or makes any sign of laughing very rarely so that most of those at court say that they have only seen him laugh once."

Catherine learned a lot about her new country in the first years of her marriage. King Francis felt it was important to be seen by his subjects far and wide, and Catherine traveled with him and his court, a group of soldiers, administrators, diplomats, and household servants. The king's entourage sometimes totaled more than ten thousand people. Francis provided several thousand horses for the most important members of the court, wagons for the women, and barges to get them all across the many rivers of France. The rest of the company traveled by foot. On these trips, Catherine was introduced to the French people and countryside. She became knowledgeable about who was loyal to the king and who schemed against him.

There were three principal parties among the high nobility at court. The first was the Bourbons, who were related to the ruling Valois family and were called Princes of the Blood because they would become heirs to the throne if the Valois line died out. Antoine of Navarre was the oldest of the Princes of the Blood and the first Bourbon in line to inherit the throne of France. His wife was the queen of

The three Guise brothers. The duke is pictured at the center and the cardinal of Lorraine is to the right. *(Château, Blois)*

Navarre, a small state in the southwest corner of France. Antoine's main preoccupation was trying to regain the portion of Navarre claimed by Spain. The second member of the Bourbon family in the line of succession was Antoine's younger brother Louis, Prince of Condé. This brother, called Condé, was an ambitious man and a strong leader.

The second powerful party at court was the Guise family. Under Francis I, the Guises had become very wealthy. Francis had also granted them titles of nobility. The Guises bragged about their French ancestry but played down the fact that they were also descended from the English House of Lorraine. England was a longtime enemy of France. The leader of the family, François, Duke of Guise, had won the respect of the king and the French people with his military skills. His brother Charles, cardinal of Lorraine, was a highly cultured and influential churchman.

The third significant party at court was the Montmorency family. The head of the family was Anne de Montmorency, the supreme military commander of France. Another important member of the Montmorency family was Gaspard de Coligny, an admiral in the French navy. The Montmorency family and the Guise family were bitter rivals. One longstanding issue in the conflict was their different attitudes toward war. The Montmorency family tended to support mediation and negotiation before resorting to violence; the Guises were more likely to support military intervention.

Catherine soon learned that these three families constantly vied for power and influence at court and in the country. There were few noblemen who were not attached in some alliance to one of the families. It was also clearly impossible for a monarch to satisfy all three political houses. All he could hope to do was skillfully play their interests against each other in hopes of limiting their ability to make mischief.

But Catherine's primary concern during her first decade in France had little to do with court intrigue. Although it was determined to everyone's satisfaction that she and Henry had consummated their marriage, the couple had yet to produce a child.

While her lack of offspring was considered a failure, it did not become critical until 1536, when a sudden, tragic event altered the course of her life forever. During the hot summer Henry's older brother, François, heir to the throne, died. He had been playing tennis in the heat and drank a glass of water to cool off. He became ill and died days later. The water-bearer at the tennis courts was an Italian, and though many believed he was innocent, the man was sentenced to death. His execution was carried out by having his body torn to pieces. Soon the rumor spread that Catherine had hired him to poison François's water. The gossips said everyone knew that Medicis used the *morceau Italianizé* to get rid of people who stood in their way. Now Henry was next in line for the crown, which meant Catherine would become queen.

The pressure on Catherine to have children increased dramatically now that her husband was the future king. After three years of marriage she had not yet conceived. When Henry claimed that a child born to a young woman at court was his, people quickly speculated that Catherine was barren. For several years she endured examinations, diets, and potions, all vain attempts to become pregnant.

It was a trying time, but Catherine revealed her political acumen in how she responded to the situation. She asked for an audience with King Francis and threw herself at his feet. She apologized for failing to produce an heir and promised to do whatever the king thought was best. She would even leave France, or join a convent, if Francis wanted her to. Or she would remain with her husband and continue trying to fulfill her childbearing mission. It was up to the king to decide the best course.

As she no doubt knew he would, the king found Catherine's deference flattering. He told her that he wanted her to remain in France as the wife of his heir. It was later reported that her valor even brought a tear to his eye. After this demonstration, Catherine's position at court was secure. She knew that Henry would jump at the chance to have her removed, but Catherine had preempted him. Even if Henry tried to rid himself of Catherine, the king would never allow it. Catherine had learned an important lesson—there was more than one way to get what she wanted.

Catherine began to look for supporters in the court. When Henry was king, she would need advisors who would help her watch out for her interests. She also watched out for Henry's interests and, although they were far from close, he slowly began to realize that Catherine's intelligence and savvy were valuable resources.

In 1538, Henry, who had been privately and publicly indifferent toward Catherine for several years, brought his mistress, Diane de Poitiers, to the castle. Diane, a widow nearly twenty years older than Henry, was not a traditionally beautiful woman, nor was she particularly intelligent. But Henry loved her intensely.

The improbable relationship between Henry and Diane de Poitiers had its roots, as did so much of Henry's life, in the five years he was held in Spain. His mother had died before he was handed over as a hostage; then he suffered the pain of being abandoned by his father. It was when the teenaged Henry returned to Paris that he first met Diane. At first, their relationship was probably more one of a surrogate mother to a motherless boy. At some point, however, it became a romantic entanglement that lasted all of Henry's life.

It was rumored that a jealous Catherine drilled a hole in the floor of her apartment, which was directly above Diane's boudoir. On the evenings when she knew that Henry was visiting Diane, Catherine had only to move a desk and pull up a rug to see what was going on below her.

Catherine's humiliation was more than just personal and

sexual, however. It was Diane who was on Henry's arm as he moved about his court and at social occasions. Catherine was always gracious and smiling, and revealed none of the humiliation that she must have been feeling. She never mentioned the entwined letters D and H that Henry had sewn on royal furniture and burned into pottery throughout the kingdom. The letters should have been C and H as

Diane de Poitiers, Henry's mistress.

custom decreed for a royal couple.

Diane was also closely aligned with the Guise family, and, with her encouragement, Henry soon came to favor that group. The Guises earned Catherine's lasting hatred when they prompted Diane to suggest that Henry

Catherine's close friend, Anne de Montmorency.

divorce his wife to marry her. Threatened by the Guise family, Catherine sought comfort from Anne de Montmorency, who became one of her closest confidantes. These early allegiances would have significant repercussions.

But Catherine's pain was not merely political. She seems to have truly loved Henry. There were reports of her sobbing at night as Henry and Diane romped one floor below. But she endured her pain without comment, regardless of how deeply she felt the humiliation as the court and populace relished her pain and openly scorned the Italian interloper who could not keep her husband happy—or bear him a child.

Catherine's life during her first ten years in France was not all suffering. She slowly began to impress the nobles and foreign dignitaries who frequented the court. The Venetian

Lorenzo Contari wrote home that "[Catherine] possesses extraordinary wisdom and prudence; there is no doubt that she would be adept at governing."

Catherine's first son, Francis.

Then, over ten years after her wedding, in January 1544, Catherine finally gave birth to a son. She had been declared sterile by court doctors years before, and the pregnancy could have given her an opportunity to gloat. Instead, Catherine gave thanks for her son and named him Francis after his grandfather, who rejoiced at the news of his birth.

The royal baptism of Francis was a glorious pageant. It opened with three hundred torchbearers lining the route from the king's apartment. Hundreds of gentlemen marched in procession to the church, which was decorated with the finest royal tapestries. A year later a girl, Elizabeth, was born. The next year Claude, another girl, arrived.

Meanwhile, the king was unwell. He was only fifty-four when his health began to fail. Exhausted from years of war, sorting out the intrigues in his court, and having to deal with the growing Protestant revolt, he lost some of the vigor that had been his most attractive feature. He admitted to Henry that he had wasted time and strength fighting unnecessary wars.

During the winter of 1546-47, King Francis was often bedridden. He would rally for a short while, then become ill again. Then, on March 29, 1547, after making his last confession and admonishing Henry to preserve the Catholic faith, he died. As his coffin was lowered into a vault, the people cried "Le Roi est mort! Vive le Roi!" King Francis was dead, long live King Henry II. The cheer did not mention the new queen.

3

Queen of France

Henry was crowned King Henry II in the Cathedral of Reims in July 1547. Catherine was not crowned queen at the time. As was traditional in France, her ceremony would come at a later date. Henry's personality seemed to change the minute the crown was placed on his head. He was not as silent, morose and unapproachable. One friend even described him as jolly and happy. One reason for his happiness was that he and the Guise family were finally able to go to war.

The Protestant Reformation, led by Martin Luther, had begun in Germany. Ever since Luther announced a break with the Catholic Church (the word "Protestant" comes from the fact that Protestants "protested" the Catholic Church's policies), religious tension and violence had spread rapidly across Europe. The terrifying sack of Rome that

Catherine's husband, King Henry II.

Catherine had lived through in 1527 was precipitated by religious differences—the army that had sought to murder the pope was made up mostly of German Lutherans.

Many French citizens were also unhappy with the Catholic Church, believing it to be a corrupt institution using its power to enrich its own coffers at the expense of the very people it purported to help. The church was seen as elitist, and its strength threatened the secular rulers of the land. A movement to reform the Catholic Church began in France. Margaret of Angoulême, the sister of Francis I, was an early convert to the Reform movement in France. She provided protection to the humanistic

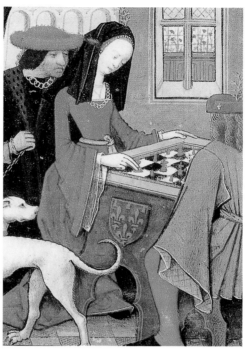

Margaret of Angoulême is depicted here as a young woman, playing chess with her brother Francis.

writers and ministers that criticized the Catholic Church on matters of doctrine as well as practice. But there were some people who did not think reform was the answer. They were inspired by Luther's example of breaking with the Catholic Church completely. One such person was John Calvin.

Born in 1509, Calvin was the son of a lawyer and administrator in the Catholic Church. Calvin was trained in the law, as well, and eventually joined his father in advocating for church reform. When Francis I began to crack down on the reformers in 1530, throwing several in prison for heresy, Calvin fled France and began a period of traveling around Europe.

By 1536, when Calvin settled in the small city of Geneva Switzerland, he had become a committed Protestant. He had earned a reputation as a theologian and writer and was persuaded to remain in Geneva, which had recently overthrown its Catholic rulers, to help establish a Protestant church and government in the city. Calvin spent most of the remainder of his life there. Although his position was merely that of a pastor in a church, Calvin's ideas and organizational genius turned Geneva into the "Protestant Rome," a theocratic city-state that provided the home base for the spread of Calvinistic Protestantism throughout Europe.

Theologically, Calvin fundamentally agreed with Luther that spiritual authority came exclusively from God. Men were saved by salvation alone, not by good works or the intercession of saints. The principal theological difference between Luther and Calvin was Calvin's doctrine of predestination. Calvin spent years elaborating on predestination, and it is a highly complicated topic. Generally, Luther believed that it was possible for all believers to experience God's grace, or salvation. Calvin, on the other hand, wrote that because God was all-knowing and all-powerful, those who were condemned were already condemned and those who were saved, whom he called the elect, were already saved. There was nothing one could do to win God's grace, according to Calvin—the decision was made long before one's birth. The elect were God's instruments whose duty it was to see that all humans, condemned and saved alike, obey God's law on Earth. God's elect were to carry out their duties in the world and challenge evil as soldiers in God's army.

John Calvin in his study.

Because his message had to be spread clandestinely, Calvin organized a church structure. Individual congregations were organized into presbyteries. Elders from each church were chosen to run the presbytery. The synod was a collection of presbyteries, and above that was a national assembly, which was the court of final authority to settle

disputes within synods or presbyteries. This cellular structure, organized around central doctrines, gave Calvinism a
unity of message and structure not found in Lutheranism.
It also made it much harder for Catholic rulers to stamp it
out. Sometimes individual congregations did not know of
the existence of congregations in the next village. Messages
could be sent quickly through the secret groups who often met
to worship clandestinely in homes or barns. This system of
underground institutions allowed for the rapid dispersal of a
powerful Protestant message throughout France.

Calvinists in France came to be called Huguenots (ex-
planations for the origin of the term vary), and their movement grew rapidly in the 1530s. The citizens of France were
fed up with the Catholic Church, which many saw as an
oppressive and repressive institution. Nearly everyone in
France agreed the church was corrupt, but they disagreed
about how to enact reform. Catholicism was the official
state religion, which meant the kings of France were closely
tied to Rome. The church was exempt from paying taxes and
had, over the years, become an extremely powerful force in
politics—the Guise family, who had enormous influence over
Catherine's husband Henry, was famous for their strict adher-
ence to Catholicism.

Before Francis died, he had been pressured by the Guises
to crack down on the emerging Huguenot presence in
France. Henry was eager to pick up where his father had left
off and to expand the persecution of religious dissidents.
But he had been warned by his father not to cede too much
power to the Guise family, so he appointed the Duke of

Montmorency Grand Marshal and gave him the authority to destroy the Protestants. The Guises were angry. They wanted to lead the fight themselves. Their thwarted desire for power would haunt the politics of France for years to come.

In 1549, when she was thirty, Catherine's fourth child and second son Louis died. He was only eight months old. In 1550, she gave birth to her third son, Charles Maximilian. Shortly after his birth, Catherine noted that there was an eclipse of the sun. She wondered if this was a sign of impending doom for little Charles. The next year another son came—this one, named Henry after his father, would be Catherine's favorite.

Diane attended the births of each of Catherine's children. Catherine may have been humiliated by the presence of her husband's adored mistress, but Diane was also an immense help. She helped supervise the children's nurses and managed other parts of their upbringing.

Catherine was having children at such a rate she certainly needed help. In 1555, Hercule was born. He was Catherine's eighth child and fourth son. Although many in France were still suspicious of Catherine's foreign status and heritage, she was more than fulfilling her assigned role of producing children. With each new baby, her ambition to influence France's destiny grew.

In spite of her many pregnancies and role overseeing a busy household, Catherine managed to find time for her interest in the arts. She invited men and women of the court to her *cercle,* a group she gathered to talk about arts and cultural matters. At these *cercles,* Catherine revived her interest in the world of the Renaissance that she remembered from her childhood in Florence and Rome. They discussed Italian painters, artists, architects, and sculptors. There were also readings and analysis of the writings of Niccolò Machiavelli and other philosophers, as well as the theory put forth in the recently published book by the Polish astronomer Nicholas Copernicus, who daringly declared that the earth revolved around the sun. Machiavelli was especially important to Catherine: his most famous work, *The Prince,* would serve as her touchstone as she fought to gain power over France.

Henry gave Catherine a castle at Montceaux-en-Brie that included an area in the garden for playing *pall-mall,* a game like croquet. She wanted to create a building on the grounds that people would talk about, to bring some of the architectural glory of Italy to her adopted country. She decided to enclose the area so that they could play pall-mall in all kinds of weather. Instead of simply building a roof over the game area, she commissioned a tall two-story building standing on a base made to look like natural rock. She included a seating area for spectators. The structure received the attention she had wanted.

Catherine also built a residence near the Louvre, the main royal castle, which she named the Tuileries. She planned for it to be a vast palace with three courtyards with magnificent flowerbeds, canals, grottoes, glazed pottery animals, avenues of trees, and an aviary. However, the architect would not comply with her plans. After a few years, Catherine gave up on the project. Legend says that she gave up on the advice

Copernicus's book *On the Revolution of Celestial Spheres* introduced the idea that the Earth rotated around the sun.

of a fortuneteller who told her that she must stay away from the construction of the Tuileries buildings if she wanted to live a long life.

Besides communing with fortunetellers, Catherine continued to consult astrology books and her astrologer, Cosimo Ruggieri, who had come from Italy to France with her. She also patronized the astrologer Nostradamus, whose predictions are still studied today. Above all, Catherine retained a loyalty to her Italian roots, and welcomed Italians, many of them political exiles, to France. Whenever possible, she gave them jobs. As more and more Italians came to France, it revived her critics, who begrudged the foreigners at court.

In 1552, under pressure from the Guises, Henry left to lead his troops against the Germans. As tradition required, he appointed Catherine as regent in his absence. If he did not return, she would supervise the crown until her son was old enough to assume it. Catherine eagerly accepted the title, but then learned that it was virtually meaningless because all her decisions had to be ratified by a majority of the Royal Council. She objected, but no one cared. Still, Catherine took her new role very seriously. She dedicated herself to the study of ruling: "I am going to be a past master at it; for from one hour to the next I study only this," she declared.

Catherine took Machiavelli as her main teacher. His book *The Prince* outlined what some consider to be devious or unscrupulous methods of obtaining and maintaining power. Some believe *The Prince* to be a satire of the Medici family (though the book was dedicated to Catherine's father), others see it as serious political tome. Either way, Catherine seemed to take Machiavelli's messages to heart. One passage explained that a leader "who wishes to maintain the state is often forced to do evil." Another declared: "it is better to be impetuous than cautious, for fortune is a woman and it is necessary . . . to conquer her by force." Catherine next studied the documents that gave her the authority of a regent and learned that her duties included meeting with the king's council, maintaining communication with ambassadors, keeping an eye out for possible uprisings in Paris, and raising funds to support the king's army. She decided to focus on these responsibilities. It would be a way to build her authority.

To call attention to Henry's absence and her role as regent, she dressed in mourning all the time that he was gone and requested that the other women in her court do the same. She sent frequent letters to her husband assuring him of her desire to please him. She received no letters in return. Henry wrote his letters to Diane.

The fight with the Germans waxed and waned. Henry won some battles, lost others, advanced and retreated. France's old enemy, Holy Roman Emperor Charles V, gave most of his power to his son, Philip, who continued his father's wars. As King Philip II of Spain, he sent troops against the French in 1557. Henry put François, the Duke of Guise and the cardinal of Lorraine in charge of his military forces. He had been pleased by Catherine's fundraising skills and asked her to obtain needed war funds from the Estates General, the French parliament that was seldom called into session.

For the first time in her life, Catherine addressed a large gathering. She created drama from her first steps into the building, dressed in her black mourning clothes, surrounded by her court who was also in mourning dress. She told members of the Estates General that France was close to death, that only they could resuscitate the kingdom. She begged for 300,000 francs, telling her spellbound audience that the alternative was a humbled country. When they voted for the funds, she thanked them graciously.

Catherine owed her political victory to her touch for the dramatic and also to her clear and open enthusiasm for Henry and for France. That a foreigner who was constantly embarrassed by her husband's infidelity would still speak so eloquently about the need to raise money to protect France made an impact on the members of the Estates General.

With renewed funding, the French army was able to stop the Spanish progress into France. There was no doubt in the minds of anyone, including Catherine, that she had saved France. Because of her intelligence, modesty, and patriotic devotion, Catherine suddenly surpassed both her husband and his mistress in popularity. One ambassador wrote, "she is so much loved that it is almost unbelievable."

But Catherine still faced opposition. The Duke of Guise, who had cast his lot with Diane, was one of her most vocal critics. He said that the French had conceded too much in the peace agreement. He was not interested in Catherine's argument that peace was better than continuing the war. He was interested only in assuring that Catherine did not usurp the authority he wanted for himself and his family. Guise was determined that his family would rule France one day and was willing to destroy anyone he felt was in his way. Catherine had not forgotten that the Guises had encouraged

Henry to divorce her—she knew they were dangerous. The only weapons Catherine had in her fight for power were her cunning and her children.

In 1558, the French fought England over the port of Calais in a war that ended indecisively. In the same year, Francis, the dauphin was married

The Duke of Guise. *(Bibliothèque Nationale, Paris)*

to Mary Stuart (Mary Queen of Scots), the daughter of Mary of Guise and King James V of Scotland. Henry hoped this marriage, which he had arranged when King James died in 1542, would forge a useful political alliance for France. The Guise family encouraged the union since Mary Stuart was one of their own. Catherine opposed the idea but Henry did not listen to her arguments. He boasted that he was able to persuade Mary's family to agree that if she died without children, she would deed Scotland to France, as well as her claim to the crown of England. Catherine knew Mary's presence would strengthen the Guises' power over the throne.

Soon after the arrival of Mary Stuart in France, hostilities between France and Spain resumed. The conflict was again over territory. Spain had seized part of the province of Navarre, which was ruled by the Bourbons, cousins of the Valois. Though Navarre had its own king, parts of it were also claimed by France and Spain. The Duke of Guise was once again leading the French troops. The fighting dragged on for months. The Guises were determined to finish the war with a decisive victory that would bestow glory on their family. Catherine begged her husband to end the fighting. Had not King Francis admitted on his deathbed that he regretted all the wasteful wars he had engaged in during his reign? Henry resisted Catherine's advice for as long as he could but finally had to admit she was right. The treasury was empty and he could not ask for more taxes to pursue this war.

On April 3, 1559, Henry and Philip II of Spain signed a treaty that ended the war neither side could afford to continue. In the Treaty of Cateau-Cambrésis, Henry agreed to renounce all claims to Italy and in return was allowed to keep the cities of Metz and Calais. The Guises were furious: "you [Henry] have given away more in one day than we could have lost for you in thirty years." Included in the treaty were arranged marriages intended to bring the parties together in peace, most importantly the betrothal of Eliza-beth, Catherine and Henry's oldest daughter, to Philip II, a widower. The arrangement of the marriage was typical; Elizabeth's objections were not. She complained that the intended groom was too old and that she did not want to live in Spain. Her objections fell on deaf ears.

Two months after the peace treaty was signed, fourteen-year-old Elizabeth was married by proxy to Philip and proclaimed queen of Spain. There were many days of celebrations, which included parties and balls, sports contests and dances. Henry became so involved in the sports events that he challenged one of the best lancers to a duel. Victory would be announced for the fighter who, without being unhorsed, broke three lances against the armor of his opponent.

Catherine begged her husband not to fight—a decade before, the astrologer Ruggieri had predicted Henry would die in just such a scenario. But Henry had dismissed

Catherine spectates at one of the tournaments in celebration of Elizabeth's marriage.

Ruggieri's claims as nonsense, and now he brushed off Catherine's objections. Wearing the colors of his mistress Diane, Henry rode to the lists. His opponent, a wealthy young Huguenot, thrust his lance at Henry's face, piercing his visor and going through his eye and into his brain.

The king was carried from the field with a long splinter jutting from his helmet. Doctors were summoned, and when they could not agree on how to remove the pieces of the lance, Catherine had several criminals—already condemned to die—executed that night so that their skulls could be examined in an effort to save Henry. For ten days he drifted in and out of consciousness and pain. Catherine remained at his bedside day and night. Doctors were able to remove some splinters from the wound, but not all of them. After two weeks in a coma, King Henry II died on July 10, 1559.

Despite the ill treatment she had received from Henry, Catherine was grief-stricken. For the prescribed forty days of mourning, she remained in black clothes and these, combined with a new weight gain, gave her an unhealthy look. Relatives and friends who tried to comfort her said that she spoke "in such a feeble voice that it was difficult to understand. . . . she had a black veil on her head which covered her completely even to her face." She told them that she was learning the importance of "conforming myself to the will of God and accepting everything as coming from His hand."

Fifteen-year-old Francis was not prepared emotionally or intellectually to rule, although he was technically of age. The Guise family, seeing their chance, argued that Francis would need a regent until he was old enough to rule by

Catherine in black mourning clothes.

himself. They would be happy to take on the responsibility. Without consulting Catherine, the Duke of Guise and the cardinal of Lorraine took charge of the kingdom. Catherine was simply the widow of the former king, and those who wanted to seize power assumed she could be ignored.

Guise and Lorraine moved quickly to dispose of any opposition to their plans. They ordered Montmorency to guard the king's body. They took Francis to the Louvre and placed him under twenty-four-hour guard. They forced

Diane to hand over the crown jewels, assuming correctly that she would permanently leave the court, and they established themselves as rulers of France, ignoring the fact that the king of Navarre, Antoine of Bourbon, was, by Salic Law, next after Francis in the line of ascension. (Salic law stated that the throne should go to the man who could trace his lineage in the male line to a kingly ancestor to whom the reigning king was also related.)

In September 1559, Francis was crowned king of France in the Cathedral of Reims. Spectators reported that the ceremony was formally correct, but lacked the joy that usually attended a coronation. It was obvious to all that Francis was not physically, intellectually, or emotionally strong enough to rule the country. The Guises persuaded the newly crowned Francis II to place himself in their hands and Catherine acquiesced. France had passed into Guise control.

Catherine's devotion to her husband continued after his death, and her only desire was to ensure that his descendants would continue to rule France well into the future. She allowed the Guises to supervise Francis's reign because she thought they might help her to achieve her own long-term ambitions. The Guises could help her by thwarting the ambitions of the Bourbons. Catherine would devote the rest of her life to trying to unify France and end the religious wars splintering the country so that her progeny might bring glory to the throne. Though she had little to work with—her children were mostly weak, her powers were limited by her gender and her foreign status, and France was divided under rival powers—she never gave up her relentless pursuit of power.

4

So Much Blood

The Guises, now in effective control of the government, found themselves in a difficult situation. The long series of wars had almost ruined the country. The treasury was empty—even the interest on the national debt went unpaid—and the people could not bear more taxes. There was widespread corruption and inefficiency, salaries of thousands of government workers had not been paid for four years, and the army was drastically reduced.

The most pressing problem, however, was the religious conflict between the Protestant Huguenots and the Catholics. Although he did engage in sporadic attacks on Protestant meetings and executed suspected leaders, King Francis I had managed to avoid wholesale civil war by twice issuing edicts that proclaimed that religious heresy no longer existed in France. All the "former" heretics had to do was attend mass and confession, return to the Catholic fold, and all would be forgotten. The Duke of Guise, who had established his family as the champions of the Catholic faith, had grumbled that Francis was failing in his duty to protect his people from heresy—that by refusing to destroy it he was allowing it to spread.

When Henry II had come to power, the Duke of Guise convinced him to institute a policy of severe persecution. Henry declared that it was time to eradicate the Protestant scourge forever. Catherine, who never wavered in her devotion to Catholicism, had nevertheless argued futilely that it was not wise to attempt to fight a war against heresy and a war against Spain at the same time.

Henry had created courts to hear heresy cases. A "trial" in these courts was actually an interrogation. The suspected heretic was asked a series of questions while being tortured by a variety of methods, including having molten metal poured over his feet or sharp objects driven into soft parts of his body. A mere accusation in open court that someone was a heretic was all it took to bring someone to trial.

The Guises pushed constantly for a more energetic effort to round up Huguenots. Although they were staunch Catholics, the Guises also had another motivation to press the issue. Antoine, the king of Navarre, who was a Prince of the Blood and technically in line for the crown, was rumored to be a Protestant. It was said that he attended both Huguenot meetings and Catholic Mass. While no one knew for certain whether Antoine was Protestant, his brother Louis, Prince of Condé, was openly one of the most important Huguenot leaders. By persecuting Protestants, Guise could undermine the Bourbon family's claim to the throne.

Henry had been convinced to proclaim that Protestant church services were acts of treason against the state. He had ordered the death penalty be applied to anyone hold-

Louis, Prince of Condé.

ing such worship services, as well as the wholesale arrest and imprisonment of all Protestants. But Henry's efforts to end Protestantism in France had only created martyrs, which added more fuel to the Huguenot cause.

When the sickly and immature Francis II became king, the Guises were given free reign. They intensified religious persecution. Catherine hoped her son would grow stronger and mature with age, but Francis seemed to only grow weaker, both in spirit and in health. He seemed confused by his role—or lack of it—in the government. He was listless and cared only for hunting. Catherine despaired as she watched him fall further into Guise control. By late 1559, Catherine was at her nadir in influence; she seemed to be losing everything. She was a widow, her son was under the power of another family, her beloved daughter Elizabeth lived in Spain with the still-hated Philip II, and she had lost an infant son. But she remained determined to play a role in the affairs of France.

Catherine warned the Guises against the continuing religious persecution. Catherine's argument was based on practical reasons, not moral ones. She believed it was most urgent to train the king to assume power, replenish the treasury, and restore the economy after the decades of war. But the Guises, of course, had no intention of slowing down. The increased persecutions only served to strengthen the Huguenot resistance. With the help of Protestant Queen Elizabeth I of England, a group of French Huguenots devised a plot to seize the Guise leaders and either imprison or kill them. They enlisted the help of the adventurer Jean de Barry.

De Barry pretended he was organizing a delegation of loyal subjects who would meet to call on King Francis II to ask for redress of economic hardships brought on by the war. His real plan was to arrest the Duke of Guise and his brother, the cardinal of Lorraine, and either try them in court or kill them outright. When spies brought word of the plot to Lorraine, the cardinal and his brother were delighted to learn that the Bourbon Condé was involved.

On February 1, 1560, the Guise court, along with the king, took up residence at the castle Blois on the Loire river. Francis II had planned a few weeks of hunting, away from the politics of Paris. The Huguenot plotters saw this as a perfect time to attack. They were thwarted when, on February 6, Lorraine shocked the assembled court by announcing that he had uncovered a plot to kill the king. Catherine too had heard rumors of de Barry's recruitment of citizens to petition the king, and she feared for her son's life. She began to assemble a force of her own to protect Francis.

The Guises had planned to use the plot to their advantage. After the cardinal of Lorraine's announcement, the Duke of Guise said that the court must move immediately to Amboise, a town on the other side of the Loire, where there was more protection. Taken by surprise by the move of the court, de Barry postponed his own plans until February 16. However, his supporters did not get the notice to delay the plot right away. Guise spies learned of the change before some of de Barry's fellow conspirators did. When some of the plotters showed up at the castle on the original date of the ambush, they were immediately overwhelmed. The rest of the ill-fated conspirators were soon rounded up. The arrested men were interrogated, forced to give names of their co-conspirators, and tortured. What became known as the Conspiracy of Amboise had been ruthlessly aborted.

The Guises resolved to use the opportunity to teach a lesson the Protestants would never forget. Some of those conspirators who were still alive after interrogation were dragged to the castle at Amboise where they were publicly tortured and dismembered and thrown in the Loire. Then days of public execution, to be held in the courtyard of the castle at Amboise, were announced and special masses said. In the end, fifty-seven executions were attended and applauded by Catherine, King Francis II, the cardinal of

This anonymous engraving shows the execution of the Amboise conspirators on March 15, 1560. A crowd of more than 10,000 onlookers came to glimpse the carnage.

Lorraine, the Duke of Guise, Mary Stuart, Catherine's second son Charles, and a papal emissary.

Condé was also forced to attend. Guise had hoped that one of the conspirators would break in the torture and name Condé as their leader, but none did. Condé stood ramrod straight as his Protestant brethren mounted the scaffold. It was reported that he looked each man in the eye and gave each one a single, almost imperceptible nod, before the victim lowered his head for the executioner's axe. The killing went on for nine days. The courtyard became so full of blood that finally Guise's own wife broke down and was heard to scream "My sweet God, so much blood. Surely some of it will fall upon our house," as she was carried away.

The public reaction to the executions at Amboise was similarly strong. Catherine was castigated by anonymous pamphleteers, who portrayed her as an evil murderess gloating over the bodies of the conspirators. The reputation of Catherine de' Medici that has captured imaginations throughout history was initially forged after the Conspiracy of Amboise. Later events would harden it even further.

In the meantime, the Guises continued their campaign against the Huguenots and the Bourbons. They were determined to establish themselves as the protectors of the Catholic faith—which would win them valuable papal support in any showdown over the French throne—and to remove the Bourbons from the line of succession.

The summer of 1559 was marked by increased hostility and violence. Protestants were hunted down and their makeshift meeting places destroyed. In some towns and villages, pictures of the Virgin Mary were placed on busy streets and corners. Anyone who refused to kneel before the Virgin was arrested for heresy.

Frustrated at their failure to implicate Condé, Guise and his brother, the cardinal of Lorraine, decided to call a meeting of the Estates General to be held in Orléans. Their ostensible reason to call the assembly was to discuss the growing religious conflict. Their actual plan was to entice Condé and his brother, Antoine, the king of Navarre, to Paris in order to arrest them. Navarre would be held to keep him from rallying to his brother's defense until the Guises could convince Francis to have Condé beheaded. The brothers initially refused to come to Orléans, even when Catherine herself asked them to. It was only after the cardinal of Lorraine gave them a written guarantee of safe passage that they agreed to attend the Estates General.

On their first day in Orléans, Condé and Antoine were arrested and thrown into prison. Because he was the ruling monarch of Navarre, and a Prince of the Blood, Antoine was later released and put under house arrest. But Condé remained in prison and Guise began to plan his elimination. Meanwhile, the other delegates to the assembly were given declarations of the faith that they were to take back to their provinces and make sure all public officials signed. Anyone who refused to sign would be arrested. Guise and Lorraine were convinced this would wipe out Protestantism.

Then fate intervened. After witnessing the executions at Amboise, King Francis II had spent most of his time hunting. Winter was approaching and he was spending most of his waking hours in the forest on horseback. It was as though he would do anything to avoid tending to his state duties. The king became sick in November, complaining of a violent headache, so acute he could not bear the slightest noise. His wife, Mary, and his mother attended him almost constantly but could do little to alleviate his suffering.

Once it was clear that Francis was not improving, Catherine rode through heavy snows to meet with the astrologer Nostradamus. He had been away from her court for many years but had promised he would always come if she called him. Now, she needed his help.

Nostradamus used magic circles and chants to reveal the future in a mirror. Catherine was shocked by what she saw there. The prophecy was that Francis would die soon, and that Charles would succeed him, reign fourteen years, then be replaced by his next brother, Henry. But when Henry's

Catherine consulting with the legendary Nostradamus about the future of the Valois family. *(Bibliothèque Nationale, Paris)*

reign was over, Catherine was amazed to see not her next son on the throne, but the young son of Antoine of Navarre. This prophecy meant that all Catherine's work to keep the throne of France for her family would fail when the Valois line was replaced by the Bourbons. Catherine's strong belief in the prediction she was given that day would influence her future actions. For now, she concentrated on establishing herself as regent for ten-year-old Charles because she knew Francis's death was near.

Tradition dictated that a council headed by the First Prince of the Blood, King Antoine of Navarre in this case, would rule until the heir to the throne was old enough to take over. But Catherine was not going to allow the Bourbons to get their hands on the crown. Not only did she want the power of the throne for herself and her children, but she knew that a Bourbon regency would throw the country into a civil war. The Catholic Guises would not give up their power quietly.

By seizing Navarre and Condé, the Guise family had unwittingly made it easier for her to control the situation to her advantage. She called Antoine to her and reminded him that he was still officially under arrest for his plotting at Amboise and for heresy. The entire Bourbon family was in disgrace. Her message was clear—Antoine was in no position to challenge her regency.

Then, as Machiavelli would have recommended, she softened the blow. Out of the kindness of her heart, she said, and in appreciation for his years of service to her husband and son, Catherine offered to appoint him to the prestigious job of Lieutenant General of the kingdom. This was a high military honor that would help Antoine to protect his family from the Guises' treachery. It was a shrewd political move. Antoine felt cheated, and was bitter, but under the circumstances he could not protest. He had to take what he could get. Catherine left nothing to chance and assigned two of her ladies-in-waiting to spy on Antoine.

While Catherine negotiated the future, Francis continued to decline. He was too frail to stand straight, his eyes watered constantly, and he was sickly pale. There was a huge open sore behind his ear and he was in intense pain. Catherine made sure he saw only her and Mary Stuart. Together, they nursed him as well as they could.

It soon became obvious that Francis would not recover. Guise and Lorraine were anxious that Condé should not survive the king. But they could not execute him without the king's signature. Guise sent a messenger to take the order to the king but Catherine refused to allow him entry into her son's bedroom. Francis lingered near death for a month before finally succumbing on December 5, 1560. Though Catherine's life was made miserable by religious conflict, she wrote that she could not have endured the grief without her faith that her son's death was the will of God. To her daughter Elizabeth, Catherine said, "God has taken him [my husband] from me and still, not content with that, He has taken your brother . . . now I am left with three small children and a kingdom divided into factions." It was only by the strength of her faith, she added, that she was able to survive.

Catherine's ten-year-old second son was now King Charles IX. She appeared by the new king's side on December 6 and announced that she would serve as regent. The Guises were out of power.

Catherine carried through her promise of naming Navarre Lieutenant General and appeared at his

Catherine's second son, Charles, inherited the throne after the death of his brother, Francis II.

side as a way to signal he was safe and under her protection. Condé was released from prison. But, after the release of his brother, Navarre, who was seething at the turn of events, decided to retaliate. Although he had publicly acceded to Catherine's authority, Navarre disrupted the Estates General, which was still in session, and demanded more power for himself and the dismissal of the Duke of Guise from any position of power. He threatened to return to Navarre and begin raising an army if his demands were not met.

Catherine knew that if Navarre left her court he would join Condé and that the two combined, and propelled by the force of thousands of angry, persecuted Huguenots, would be a formidable enemy. But a dismissed and shamed Guise would be just as formidable a threat. She met with Navarre and asked him to reconsider his demands, but he refused. On the last day of February, he prepared to leave the court.

Suddenly Charles IX appeared at court and begged the brothers to stay in tribute to his father. For the good of all of France, the boy king said, they should put aside their personal battles and unite. Caught unaware by this call to their patriotism, Navarre agreed, with the condition that Condé be invited to court and allowed to vindicate himself.

In his appearance before the Royal Council at court, Condé swore that he had never conspired against the king. His word was accepted, although few actually believed him. Now that the threat of violence from the Bourbons had been negated, Catherine had bought a little time to restore the crown's finances and to establish herself more firmly in power. She wrote to her daughter Elizabeth, living in Spain with her husband King Philip, "Thanks be to God, I am at peace again."

Her reprieve was short-lived, however. In the middle of March, Condé returned to Paris. Once in the capital city, he claimed the queen mother had no right to the throne. The regency rightly belonged to Antoine, he said. If Antoine had rejected it, then he, Condé, would accept it. When Antoine learned that his brother was trying to outflank him and seize power, he reneged on his promise to Catherine and demanded that he be made regent. When Guise heard Navarre's demand he retorted: "There is no one in the world strong enough to chase me. Before I leave, 40,000 men will die at my feet."

If she had to choose between Guise or Navarre, Catherine would side with the more powerful and Catholic Guise. But she had no intention of letting either man remove her from power. She wanted a conciliation in which neither side would win or lose. She had heard that hundreds of Huguenots were gathered around Condé, ready to support him. She feared that if she openly supported Guise there would be civil war. For almost a week, she negotiated with both sides. Her argument was that neither could hope to rule a united France. The selection of either would result in chaos and destruction. Finally, she was reaffirmed as regent. Antoine conceded that the Duke of Guise could remain at court, and the duke conceded that Condé would have a role in the government. Of course, no one was fully satisfied with the concessions.

Despite lacking the court's confidence, Catherine was now the regent of France, ruler in everything but name. But, as she had been from birth, she was still in a dangerous and

Michel de L'Hôpital. *(Louvre, Paris)*

precarious position. She did not have the full support of either the Guises or the Princes of the Blood. Many of her subjects rejected her as a false Catholic. After the agreement with Condé, many Huguenots became more open about their worship. They demanded the right to worship publicly instead of just in their homes. Condé even held Protestant services openly in his apartment, and his older brother, the indecisive Antoine of Navarre, continued to attend both Protestant services and Catholic Mass. This led many Catholics to condemn Catherine for allowing Calvinism to spread.

Catherine still hoped to start a process that could heal the rift between Catholics and Protestants. While she was a devout Catholic, she was willing to endorse a policy of religious toleration if it meant a peaceful kingdom. History would show that policy to have been a mistake.

Catherine appointed Michel de L'Hôpital, a man held in the highest esteem by both sides for his ethics and wisdom, as chancellor (head of state). She knew that neither side would dare to oppose L'Hôpital. He suggested that Catherine call for an open council to bring together representatives of both faiths. Catherine agreed and called for a meeting to be attended by representatives from the Vatican, Calvin's head-quarters in Geneva, and the royal court. The purpose was to discuss ending the religious conflict and to seek out ways for possible reconciliation.

The council was held at Poissy, a town not far from Paris. Catherine worked hard to prepare. She had two primary goals—to protect her sons and keep them in power, and to begin the process of bringing political and religious peace to France. She saw Antoine and Condé, and Guise and Lorraine, as almost equal threats. It was important that both sides be contained. Fifty Catholic officials were sent from France and the Vatican in Rome. Calvin reluctantly agreed to send fifteen elders from Geneva.

Unsurprisingly, and despite her best efforts, the Poissy Council was a failure. Almost immediately the meeting

Present in the front row at the Poissy Council are Antoine of Navarre (E), Henry of Anjou (C), Charles IX (A), Catherine (B), Princess Margo (D), and Jeanne d'Albret, queen of Navarre (F).

disintegrated into an ugly debate. The fundamental disagreement was over the rite of communion, and it was a
disagreement that could not be resolved. Catherine's frustrations were summed up in a dry comment from the
ambassador from Venice: "I do not believe that Her Majesty
understands what the word 'dogma' means." The
ambassador's wry assessment of Catherine's failings is
revealing: Catherine saw the religious conflict as a political
problem that could be solved through negotiation. But the
truth is that it was the fundamental differences in the beliefs
of these two religions, along with the political, social, and
economic divisions of their followers, which dissolved any
possible middle ground.

In an attempt to salvage something from the council,

Admiral Gaspard de Coligny.

Catherine met with
Admiral Gaspard de
Coligny, a hero of
France who had
fought beside both
Francis I and Henry
II. Coligny had re-
cently converted to
Calvinism and, be-
cause of his good
name and heroic
past, had quickly
become a highly in-
fluential Protestant
leader. Condé, an-

other powerful Protestant, had over-played his hand by attempting not only to remove Catherine from power but by also attempting to circumvent his brother. He was young and hotheaded. Coligny, on the other hand, would never give his support to such a poorly organized plot as the Conspiracy of Amboise that had led so many young Huguenots to their death. Catherine realized that Coligny was a much more formidable foe.

Catherine had made many Catholics angry by calling the Poissy Council. Many of them, led by the Duke of Guise, had walked out. They wanted victory, not reconciliation. Guise was threatening to join forces with Philip II of Spain to remove the Valois, Catherine's family, from power. Catherine took advantage of Guise's divisive stand by joining with Coligny and a more moderate Catholic leader to issue an edict calling for religious peace until a way could be found to bring all Christian believers into one fold. This so-called Edict of Toleration was not a solution to the deep-seated problems of France. But it gave Catherine an opportunity to point out to the French people that she, unlike Guise, was working to find a way to stop the violence that lay like a pall over the land. It also deeply embittered the Duke of Guise toward Coligny.

5

Queen Mother

The Huguenots had been overjoyed at Francis II's death. They had hoped it would end the bloody repression led by the Guises and had celebrated the return of Antoine of Navarre to the royal court. John Calvin urged Antoine, who, though he changed religions six times during his life but was at this point claiming loyalty to the Protestant cause, to retain a position of leadership in France and to prevent Catherine from seizing total power. He wrote: "To consent that a widow and a foreigner and an Italian to boot should rule will not only redound to his [Antoine's] own great dishonor but to such prejudice to the crown that he will be everlastingly blamed." Others in France, even among the Catholics, agreed with Calvin that Catherine should not rule. They resented her Italian blood, her middle-class origins, and the fact that she was a woman.

The day after Francis's death, Catherine told her Council that she would make all decisions without consulting the Estates General. She assured them that she would be a great help to her son and that she would "help [him] govern the state as a loving mother should." She made it clear that the king would rule through her. She would formulate policy, make decisions, and bestow favors. The only role of the Estates General would be to raise money.

Charles IX made his first appearance as king seven days after the death of his brother. He sat in the Estates General at Orléans on a raised stage. His mother and siblings sat next to him. Some said that he looked like a small boy waiting to take his turn in a pageant. L'Hôpital opened the cer-emony by stressing the need for the rec-onciliation of Catho-lics and the follow-ers of the new reli-gion. He said: "Force and violence pertain to beasts not to men.

King Charles IX. *(Musée Condé, Chantilly)*

Justice derives from reason, that most divine part of our being." Unfortunately, the speech only served to anger Catholics and Protestants alike.

Before Francis's death, Catherine had managed to gain the support of the Royal Council, one member at a time. Now she set her sights on gaining the approval of the most powerful members of the Estates General. She tried to appease the religious factions by insisting that behind all her actions was the overwhelming desire to bring peace to the kingdom.

Yet her attempts at peace only drove the Guises and Montmorency, who had once been enemies, together. They joined another noble and general, Marshal of Saint-Andre, to form a triumvirate to protect the Catholic faith. The Huguenots responded to her Edict of Toleration by becoming even more active in defense of their faith. The tension in France had only increased—Catherine continued to underestimate the intractable nature of the combatants.

But still, she persisted. She tried to enlist leaders of both sides to mediate the conflicts. She even sent a message to John Calvin in Geneva that some of his preachers were trying to incite rebellion, hoping he would intervene. She wrote to Philip II of Spain, who was a main force behind the Catholic Church's movement to wipe out the Protestant Reformation, to warn him that violence was not an effective way to root out heresy.

The Calvinists continued to grow bolder during this period of relative tolerance. In response, the pope proposed to the triumvirate that they work with Philip of Spain to drive the heretics out of both France and Spain. Once again

Catherine tried to find a compromise that would avoid bloodshed. Because Catherine was Catholic, she could have thrown in with the Guise family, but she still believed it might be possible to salvage peace—and her own power. What she did not realize was that her power was threatened when she came across as indecisive and noncommittal.

This perception was only heightened by the Edict of Toleration that Catherine issued in 1562. It proclaimed that leaders of religions other than Catholicism could apply for the right to assemble in France. All the major Catholic leaders, including King Philip II of Spain (Catherine's son-in-law), the pope, and the Duke of Guise, believed the statement was a terrible mistake. To them, Protestant worship was heresy no matter where it took place. The Huguenots seized upon the edict as official recognition of their right to exist. This antagonized the Catholics, and protests, demonstrations, and persecution increased.

Now there was talk in Europe of armed intervention in France by the Catholic powers. Antoine of Navarre declared publicly that he had converted to Catholicism and agreed to throw his full support to the triumvirate if they supported his right to depose Catherine. He still believed that, as the First Prince of the Blood, the throne was rightfully his. Fearing for her safety and that of her children, Catherine fled to Montceaux in eastern France.

In this heated political climate, the Duke of Guise marched into Vassy, a small walled town on the route to Paris, on the first of March, 1562. While he and his armed men were attending Mass, he heard the sounds of a Protestant church service and sent some men to silence it. The Huguenots at the meeting attacked Guise's men. Guise rushed to the site with reinforcements. About fifty Huguenots were killed, and one hundred were wounded. Within three months, an open civil war had begun. The Wars of Religion would continue intermittently for thirty-six years. Brothers fought brothers, neighbors fought neighbors, until once-fertile fields were only bloody battlegrounds, rivers were polluted with the dead, and buildings were demolished.

Catherine knew the horrors of a civil war from her childhood experiences. She ordered leaders of both sides to

Many bloody massacres took place on both sides during the Wars of Religion. In this picture, Huguenots are ransacking and desecrating a Catholic church. *(Bibliothèque Nationale, Paris)*

come to court to talk but both refused. She wrote Condé a secret letter: "I see so much that upsets me . . . I hope that we shall be able to find remedy for everything with your good advice and help." She added that she sympathized with his need to take up arms. Condé published parts of the letter out of context to give the impression Catherine had urged him to take up arms.

Catherine was desperate to counter Condé's claim. She repeated over and over that she was a believing Catholic and would always remain one. But now both sides openly scorned her. The Huguenots said that she did not keep the promises she made to Condé; the Catholics were angry that she had made promises in the first place. In desperation, she wrote: "I do not see any great hope . . . I see rather the manifest loss of this whole kingdom." Without another option, she turned her back on the Huguenots and threw her support to the triumvirate. She gave them permission to use royal taxes to pay their troops and to recruit Swiss mercenaries.

The Huguenots turned to Germany and England for help. Queen Elizabeth of England offered six thousand men and money to support the Protestant cause. Protestant leaders signed a Treaty of Association to "maintain the honor of God, the peace of the kingdom, the liberty of the king under the government of the queen his mother." They declared that the aim of the Huguenots was to free Catherine, the queen mother, and her sons from the influence of the Guises. Catherine tried unsuccessfully to talk to Condé about peace. Finally she told him, "Since you rely on your forces, we will show you ours."

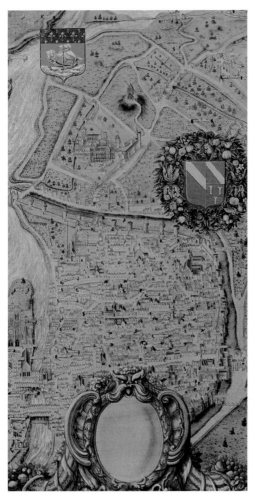

By the sixteenth century, Paris was the most densely populated city in Europe, presenting the city with unprecedented sanitation issues. *(Hôtel de Ville, Paris.)*

An exhausted Catherine returned to plague-ridden Paris where death-carts led by chanting priests rattled through the cobblestone streets day and night. Church bells tolled and people wept behind closed shutters.

Catherine ordered troops to attack the city of Rouen, located east of Paris on the Seine. Before they marched, she asked Guise to save as much of this beautiful city as possible. Rouen was home to the largest clock in Christendom and a cathedral that had taken three hundred years to build, as well as other churches and bell towers. The most sacred spot in the city, called the *donjon,* was where Joan of Arc, the charismatic peasant girl who led the French armies to lift the English siege during the Hundred Years

War, was sentenced to die at the stake. Catherine's intentions were noble, but soldiers are taught to destroy, not to save. Rouen was only one casualty of the fighting—Antoine of Navarre, who was killed during the battle, was another.

The next major battle was at the town of Dreux in the region of Normandy. Catherine awaited the outcome of the battle from twenty-five miles away. When Guise and Montmorency asked her to move farther from the fighting, she answered, "My courage is as great as yours."

Several indecisive battles were fought with few gains in territory or converts. In one skirmish, the Marshal of Saint-Andre, one of the triumvirate, was killed and Condé and Montmorency were defeated by the Catholic forces. The people of the region fled to caves with all they could carry. One onlooker wrote: "Normandy was so harassed by both Armies that the whole country was waste, and the poor Inhabitants reduced to the utmost misery."

Then a Huguenot who had pretended to convert to Catholicism mortally wounded the Duke of Guise. Catherine went to his side before he died. Guise had often opposed and humiliated her, but in his time of need he was comforted by her presence. When he died six days after the attack, Catherine issued a declaration that praised his courage and expressed public grief that "one of the greatest and worthiest ministers the King could ever be served by" was dead. After this eulogy, she made clear her next move: "It is I who will have to take command and play the captain." She called for an armistice. The triumvirate no longer existed. The Catholic party was leaderless. What moves would best serve

Catherine's goals now? Was this the time to effect a peace with the Huguenots? Or should she lead the Catholics to avenge Guise's death?

The Catholics were convinced that Coligny was behind

the assassination of Guise. They vowed to have revenge, but had to wait because Coligny had grown close to the king, who referred to the older man as his father. Although it was a subtle and canny move to develop a close relationship with the young king, Coligny was placing himself in grave danger. It was obvious to

Catherine's favorite son, Henry, Duke of Anjou.

everyone that Catherine much preferred her younger son, the Duke of Anjou, to Charles. She clearly thought Anjou would make the better king. Coligny took advantage of this rift and moved closer to Charles. He even began to advocate a war against Spain in defense of the Protestants in the Spanish-controlled Netherlands. Although to go to war against Catholic Spain in defense of Protestant rebels would be unacceptable to the Guises and would certainly throw France back into a civil war, Charles was considering the plan. Catherine was determined to keep France out of war with Spain.

She was unable to move immediately against Coligny, however, because of the growing power and influence the Guise family had over the Catholic majority. Caught between the Guises and the close relationship between Coligny and her son, she needed to find a way to assert herself in a manner that would seize everyone's attention and win the king's loyalty. Her attempt to find a way out of this dilemma was the root cause of one of the most barbarous events in European history.

But that was still almost a decade in the future. In 1563 Catherine decided that the best course of action was to declare thirteen-year-old Charles a king in his own right. France no longer needed a regency. The next year, to restore the image of the crown, and to keep her son away from Coligny, she planned to take him on a journey throughout his kingdom. She would draw the attention, and hopefully the loyalty, of the French people on a twenty-six-month, three-thousand-mile trip. Traveling mostly on horseback, she and Charles would tour the orchards of Normandy, the vineyards of Burgundy, the shores of the Mediterranean, and the wheat fields of the plains. At the end of the trip they planned to meet Catherine's daughter Elizabeth and her husband Philip II on the French-Spanish border.

While preparations for the trip were underway, Catherine called a meeting to negotiate a peace. Condé and Montmorency were invited to work on the agreement. Their recent defeat and the Duke of Guise's death made Catherine's hand stronger than it had ever been before. From the meeting came yet another edict that granted some freedom of conscience to the Huguenots in France, but regulated the right to worship according to social status, with noblemen receiving more freedom than commoners did. All property taken from the church was to be returned. The treaty would go into effect after the Council affirmed its principles. The edict was registered by the Estates General, but only reluctantly.

The treaty put an end to organized fighting for a while. Groups of conspirators continued to gather, and royal troops hunted them down, sometimes killing them on the spot and sometimes putting them through summary trials first. Catherine tried to save at least a few of the men who were condemned, but she was generally unsuccessful. Some Huguenots refused to return the church property they had confiscated. Catherine sent out twenty-eight commissioners to investigate complaints and uprisings. These were mostly ineffective. The Wars of Religion were merely paused, not finished.

The royal party began the Grand Tour in Paris in January 1564 with a retinue of hundreds of Swiss Guard, Scottish Guard, ladies of the court, barbers, secretaries, ironsmiths, and others. They took along cart after cart of furniture, tapestries, costumes for theatricals, equipment for mock tournaments, and a traveling menagerie of pets and food animals. As the travelers moved south, King Charles IX was greeted with the homage due a king. But politics were not forgotten: everywhere they went Catholics urged

Charles to act more forcefully against heretics, and Huguenots urged that he pay more attention to their complaints about intolerance.

In August, Catherine received the sad news that her daughter Elizabeth had been delivered of stillborn twins. Catherine tried to hide her grief; she had work to do. Though she was eager to see her daughter again, she had to prepare to meet with the detested Philip. She and Philip were competing for the role of protector of the Catholic Church in Europe. Catherine feared that Philip had his eyes on conquering France, which was an obstacle to his dreams of supremacy in Europe. Catherine knew she could never defeat Philip in a military conflict, so she schemed to tie him down through the bonds of marriage. In the future she hoped to marry her daughter Marguerite, called Margo, to his son Carlos; her son Edouard to Philip's sister Juana; and King Charles IX to the daughter of Philip's cousin, the Austrian emperor.

Catherine had planned for a meeting with Philip in February 1565. She was disappointed to receive word from Philip that he would not come to meet her. Instead he would send the Duke of Alva. This was an obvious insult to Catherine. The choice of substitute was particularly disturbing since Alva was known to be arrogant and inflexible. Still, Catherine met with Alva in June, and the result was as she predicted. He refused to discuss any marriages to Catherine's family until the religious conflict was resolved. He told Catherine she could solve the religious conflict by eliminating politically active Protestant leaders, rescinding all acts

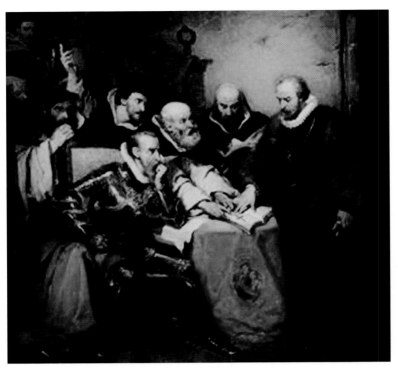

The Duke of Alva, nicknamed the "Iron Duke" because of his harsh treatment of Protestants, was the general and governor of the Spanish Netherlands from 1567-1573. He is pictured here with his advisors.

of toleration, banishing preachers who taught heresy, and making the punishment for heretics harsher. Catherine listened quietly and replied only that she heard his suggestions. She committed to nothing. For her, the only good part of the meeting was that she got to spend a few moments with her daughter.

Although by this point she had little faith that an agreement was possible, Catherine planned another council dedicated to reconciliation. This one was to be held in Moulins at the end of their journey. L'Hôpital was to preside, and Guise, Coligny, and Lorraine were invited. Once again, personal animosities flared and nothing was accomplished. Still, Catherine refused to admit defeat. She wrote: "I now live in repose and my kingdom is building up again more and more every day."

More problems with Spain arose when Philip amassed an army of ten thousand men to fight in the Spanish-controlled Netherlands after that country passed new laws recognizing the rights of Protestants. To reach the Netherlands, Philip planned to march his men through France under the leadership of the Duke of Alva.

Catherine objected to Philip's military plans. She feared that the Spanish soldiers would anger the Huguenots and possibly even attack French citizens. Charles tried in vain to convince her that they could raise an army to defeat Spain at a moment's notice if necessary. The summer of 1567 saw increased bickering between Charles and Catherine.

Philip warned her that France would suffer if she did not grant permission for his troops to cross France, but Catherine remained steadfast in her refusal. Alva went by sea, instead. He was successful at capturing the most important Protestant leaders in the Netherlands, but the fighting continued.

While Alva fought in the Netherlands it became clear that continued religious tension might lead to war in France. The fact that Catherine had met with Philip's representative was enough to enflame the Huguenots. Now that Antoine of Navarre was dead, Condé was eager to press his cause. The Protestant rebellion in the Netherlands, which was led by relatives and friends of Coligny and Condé, further emboldened the Huguenots.

A meeting was held at Coligny's castle in September 1567. He counseled patience and caution, but when word came that Catherine and Charles were in the castle at nearby Monceaux, Condé quickly organized a force to rush to the castle before royal troops arrived and seize the king and the queen mother.

When Condé's cavalry was spotted in the woods outside the castle, where Charles liked to hunt, an urgent message was sent for help. Catherine and the king fled to a nearby walled city. From there, protected by Swiss mercenaries, the royal family was able to escape to the Louvre in Paris.

Catherine was convinced that Coligny was behind the attempted kidnapping. Previously, she had hoped to work out an arrangement with him that could help to avoid bloodshed. She did not know that Coligny had tried to talk Condé out of making the attack.

Huguenot forces rushed to Paris. Frustrated at Catherine's escape, they began attacking nearby towns and even made raids into Paris. They began to steal from local shopkeepers and plundered the fields that were ready for harvest. During one battle, Constable Montmorency, who was still fighting at age seventy-five, was killed. The Huguenot forces held the field at the end of the day but were still forced to retreat because of a lack of supplies and the coming winter.

The winter was spent in a bitter stalemate. The cold weather and scarce supplies demoralized troops on both sides. Catherine called for peace and the weary leaders agreed. A treaty was signed in March, but no one expected peace to last. Neither side was satisfied with the terms. The

Continued plundering in both the towns and cities of France gave the country a feeling of great unrest.

enmity was so deep that no treaty could mend the breach. Catherine could only pray: "God will not permit this [continuing conflict]; our cause is His and that of all Christendom. He will never abandon us."

Armed conflict continued almost as though no treaty had been signed. The Catholics maintained their ruthless policies against the Huguenots, who in turn profaned altars in Catholic churches, beat priests, and tortured and mocked innocent Catholics. Soldiers roamed the countryside, restless and unpaid, responsible to no one and nothing.

For the first time since the troubles began, the Huguenots seemed to be stronger than the Catholics. They had better and more vigorous leaders, and they incited their troops with a strong sense of religious mission. The Catholics, unused to defeat, seemed irresolute. There was conflict among the leaders. Eighteen-year-old Charles lacked the charisma and experience necessary for strong leadership. Poor health and unstable emotions hindered him. Another burden faced by the Catholics was lack of money. The pope offered to allow the crown to use revenue from church lands if Catherine agreed to revoke the Edict of Toleration. Although this would only intensify the conflict, Catherine realized she had no choice but to ask Charles to issue an edict forbidding all public worship except of the Catholic faith and banishing all Protestant clergy from France.

The attempt to kidnap Charles had changed Catherine. She was now convinced that the Huguenots had no intention of agreeing to any of her attempts to reach peace. They were only interested in fomenting rebellion and putting Condé on the throne. She knew that Calvin, their spiritual leader, had been encouraging such a move. Now, Catherine's attempts at moderation were over.

6

Planning a Wedding

The Protestant leader Condé demanded that Catherine and Charles call for a new meeting of the Estates General to discuss lowering the taxes he said had been raised to enrich greedy Italians and other Catholic foreigners. It was a blatant bid for power, but Charles called the assembly and Huguenots flooded into Paris. Violence soon erupted again and spread throughout the country. The Estates General collapsed, and another round of open conflict between Catholics and Protestants ensued.

In June 1568, Catherine told a Venetian ambassador: "There are circumstances which oblige one to turn upon oneself and to submit to what one did not want in order to avoid greater ills . . . in this very room there may be people who would like to see us dead . . . but God will not allow this to happen." She also told a confidante: "I have to carry the whole burden of government alone." She was no longer interested in reaching an agreement with Condé or Coligny. The size of the royal army was increased and the order went out that all captured enemies of France would be killed.

The hastily assembled royal army was a disorganized and undisciplined group. Fortunately, the Huguenots were equally disorganized. After a single battle there was another tense period of peace.

Then, in August 1568, the longest and most awful of the religious wars began. Huguenots slaughtered women, children, and Catholic priests. They compelled monks to hang each other. At one point all the soldiers in a Catholic garrison were murdered after surrendering. Catholics attacked prisons where Huguenots were incarcerated and killed all the prisoners. In mob violence, two hundred Huguenots were tortured, burned to death, and drowned.

In September, Coligny and Condé held a meeting with other Huguenot leaders and declared that Catherine was not to be trusted. The Huguenots again marched toward Paris. Insisting that he was only trying to save the king from his wicked mother, Condé ordered the troops to loot and burn. He even had coins minted, as if he was king, bearing the inscription "Louis XIII by the grace of God, First King of the faithful of the Gospel." When Catherine learned of the coins she said, "The man has gone mad."

Over the objections of her counselors, Catherine chose her sixteen-year-old son Henry, Duke of Anjou, to be commander in chief of the royal forces. He was her favorite son and Catherine thought Anjou was the perfect leader, although he had no military experience. But he was physically stronger and more intelligent than Charles IX.

Luck was with Anjou at his first battle at Jarnac. The Catholics won a decisive victory. More importantly, Condé was killed. Impressed with his own victory, Anjou spoke out forcefully against what he considered to be the capitulation of France to the Protestants. He was ready and eager to carry on the fight and end the Protestant revolt once and for all. He became the most fearless advocate of the Catholic side, although many suspected his enthusiasm had more to do with military glory than with religious piety. His attitude created a deep chasm of mistrust between him and Charles, who feared his brother's ambitions.

Despite the victory, and the death of Condé, the Huguenots were far from being beaten. The war was consuming money and men at a furious rate. It was also beginning to divide the loyalties of the royal children. As the conflict continued, Philip II of Spain offered to send troops to aid the Catholic cause. Catherine, who knew that once Philip had implanted Spanish troops in France they would not leave voluntarily, rejected the offer. Six months after the battle of Jarnac, Anjou was victorious again, but the routed Huguenots managed to escape because King Charles IX, jealous of Anjou's victory, would not let the army pursue them. Although it was a major battlefield victory, the failure to crush the Protestant army was deeply demoralizing. The Huguenots were shaken, but not defeated. Anjou began to speak of himself as the destined leader of the Catholic cause.

After the death of Condé, Admiral Coligny became the

After many bloody battles, Anjou eventually defeated the Huguenots at the Battle of Montconcour on October 3, 1569. *(Musée de l'Histoire du Protestantisme français, Paris)*

undisputed leader of the Huguenots. He was a much more able, levelheaded leader than Condé. Until his conversion, his life had been dedicated to the service of France. Motivated more by a desire for peace that would allow Protestants to worship freely than by personal ambition, Coligny was a formidable foe. He would do what was necessary to win. The Guise family was now led by the new duke, young Henry, a sworn enemy of the Huguenots. But when Coligny's brother was poisoned, rumors spread that Catherine was behind it. Any time poison was used, the Medici queen was blamed.

After all these years of war, Catherine had to admit that all her earlier attempts to make peace had failed. She was still wary of Spain's ambitions, but as the Protestant threat grew, she decided it would be wise to strengthen ties with Philip. It seemed to be a propitious time to marry her daughter Margo to Don Carlos, Philip's heir apparent. But Philip rejected the proposal.

Catherine's daughter, Margo.

Margo, who was by far the most intelligent and capable of Catherine's children, had once been a dutiful daughter. But she had a passionate nature and wanted to marry the man she loved—not Don Carlos of Spain. Unfortunately for her, her choice was Henry, the Duke of Guise. The two first met in secret, then more openly. Margo had a reputation for promiscuity and it was rumored that she and Henry of Guise had been caught several times making love. Catherine grew tired of hearing of the affair and realized it would damage Margo's value on the marriage market. She dismissed Henry from the court. It was rumored that Charles and Catherine broke into Margo's bedroom early one morning and, after scolding her for being stubborn, beat her badly.

Another possible marriage for Margo had been arranged by her father when she was just six years old. Henry II had proposed the marriage of his daughter to Henry of Navarre, the son of then-king Antoine of Navarre. That suggestion had been made before the outbreak of the religious wars and before the Bourbons had emerged as the leaders of the Huguenots. It had seemed like the ideal arrangement, bringing together the two lines that could trace their ancestry to the founder of the French monarchy, Hugh Capet. Young Henry of Navarre had a reputation for gallivanting, but he was a Protestant, which intrigued Catherine. Catherine thought the marriage of Henry and Margo might be a way to undermine the Huguenot's leadership. Condé was now dead, and young Henry seemed impressionable. Margo was certainly beautiful enough to turn his head. What better way to attract him back into the Catholic fold than the offer of a beautiful, passionate wife and a secure position in the line of succession? Besides, Catherine never forgot the prediction of Nostradamus that Henry of Navarre would one day ascend the throne of France. If that prophecy came true, Catherine was determined to maintain her influence over the crown.

The biggest obstacle to the marriage was Henry's mother, Jeanne d'Albret. After her conversion, Jeanne had become the spiritual leader of the French Huguenot movement. She was an inspiration to thousands of French Protestants for her piety and devotion to the cause. She was opposed to her son marrying a Catholic princess with a reputation for wantonness. Furthermore, the widow of Antoine of Navarre be-

Mal sont les gens endoctrinés
quant prenne sont sermonés

Jeanne d'Albret preaching to a group of Huguenots.

lieved that Catherine had played a role in her husband's death and had been deceptive in her dealings with the Huguenots. Jeanne did not believe in religious compromise. She insisted that everyone accept the Calvinist faith. As queen of Navarre, she had ordered that Catholic churches be destroyed, nuns and priests exiled, and all Catholic ritual forbidden.

Catherine had not insisted that Henry convert in order to marry her daughter, nor would she allow Margo to give up her religion. Catherine actually liked the idea of having a Huguenot son-in-law. She had married one daughter to Philip, the king of France's long-time enemy, Spain. Marrying another to a Protestant prince seemed like a good opportunity to make a new alliance—Catherine's goal, as always, was peace, not religious domination.

Jeanne d'Albret finally gave in and agreed to the wedding. Then, suddenly, what had seemed like a victory for Catherine turned tragic. While in Paris, Jeanne returned to her quarters complaining of chest pains. Her condition continued to worsen and, on June 4, 1572, she died.

The Huguenot rage was instant. They saw the mark of the Medicis in Jeanne's death. It was said that poison had been delivered in a pair of silk gloves Catherine had given to Jeanne. Conversely, the young Duke of Guise and other Catholics believed that the hand of God had acted to stop the wedding of a Catholic and a Protestant. An autopsy revealed that Jeanne had died from lesions on her lungs, but the damage had been done.

When he learned of his mother's death, the prospective bridegroom, now King Henry of Navarre, came to Paris with eight hundred men, all wearing black mourning clothes. He was received with honor at the French court and then returned to Navarre. He surprised many of his followers, and the Guises, by not canceling the plans for his wedding.

The only stumbling block remaining was that, because he was Protestant, Henry of Navarre needed a papal dispensation before Margo could marry him. This dispensation would not be granted easily. The pope, who was actively instigating the Guises and others to take up arms against the Huguenots, would have preferred for Henry to convert. Catherine decided to not wait. She scheduled the wedding and told anyone who asked that she was sure the pope's dispensation would arrive at any moment. She then instructed her couriers not to accept any mail from Rome until after the ceremony. Fortunately for her, she found a priest to conduct the ceremony without the pope's dispensation.

The summer of 1572 was almost unbearably hot. As thousands of Protestants and Catholics flooded into Paris to attend the festivities surrounding the wedding, the hotels filled up. Sanitary facilities, always poor at best, were overwhelmed. The nineteen-year-old bridegroom rode into the city wearing black, still in mourning for his mother.

Before she died, Jeanne d'Albret had sent for Coligny and asked the admiral to protect her son. That he was marrying the sister of the king did not guarantee his safety. She also asked Coligny to keep Henry in the Protestant faith. Her husband Antoine had converted a total of six times and had last rites read to him by both a minister and a priest. It was very important to Jeanne that Henry die a Protestant.

Coligny had returned to the court in the Louvre Palace in Paris before the wedding, where he pressured Charles to go to war against Spain. Philip was still fighting a bloody Protestant revolt in the Spanish-controlled Netherlands and Coligny had made private promises to the Protestant leader, William of Orange, that he could convince Charles to declare war on France's old enemy. Charles wanted very much to lead troops into battle. His brother Anjou, who made no secret of his own lust for power, had earned his reputation by besting a poorly organized Protestant force in two battles. A victory in a war against powerful Spain, led by the young French king, would list his name among France's greatest kings. Anjou would be humbled and Charles would be loved and respected.

Catherine had long simmered that, as a result of Coligny's influence over Charles, she had not been free to move against the admiral sooner. Coligny had been instrumental in arranging the marriage of Henry of Navarre and her daughter Margo. He had been important in other ways, as a voice of reason in the Protestant camp. It had been necessary to be patient.

Once Margo and Henry's marriage was assured, Catherine was free to plot a move against Coligny. It was important that whatever was done could not be traced back to her or Anjou, who was at her side most of the time. But they needed to hurry. Charles, pressured by Coligny, was seriously considering a war with Spain. The young Duke of Guise, who blamed Coligny for the death of his father, had made it clear he would lead a revolt against the royal family if they went to war against Catholic Spain. Even the prospect of gaining wealth and territory from a French victory was not enough to entice the Guises to agree to the war. Matters were quickly coming to a head.

Catherine's first step was to drive a wedge between Charles and Coligny. In her typically manipulative fashion,

Catherine approached her goal obliquely. She visited the king, who was on a hunting trip, and asked for his permission for herself and Anjou to leave France. She told Charles that she loved him—reminding him that she had saved him from a Protestant kidnapping attempt—and that she loved France, but that she could not stand by and watch him destroy her family and her country in a war against Spain. She preyed upon Charles's jealousy of his brother by asking to be allowed to go with Henry of Anjou back to Italy. Charles reacted as she had hoped, by dropping to his knees, begging her forgiveness, and promising to reject Coligny's war with Spain. He even promised to try to patch up his tattered relationship with his brother. The old admiral had been out-maneuvered.

Still, Huguenot fighters began leaving Paris to fight on the side of the Dutch Protestants. Catherine feared that Philip would use the presence of these French fighters as an excuse to invade France. She was also concerned that a Protestant victory to the north would make France vulnerable to a Protestant invasion.

Reconciliation, it seemed, was a dangerous pipe dream. Even the wedding of Navarre and Margo was being used by the Huguenots as a way to consolidate their forces before heading out to fight the Spanish. The internal religious conflict had taken on dangerous international implications.

Catherine had to leave Paris in July 1572, days before the wedding, to attend to her ill daughter Claude, who was now the Duchess of Lorraine. Coligny took advantage of her absence to redouble his effort to convince Charles to declare war on Spain. A Spanish rout of an army of three thousand Huguenots earlier in the month had made the Protestant cause more desperate. The usually diplomatic Coligny became heated as he exhorted the king to strike the hated Spanish while they were vulnerable. Catherine returned to Paris before Coligny could fully convince Charles to go to war; but she realized that her son's vacillating nature could not be trusted. She decided the only sure path was to remove from the scene the talented and persuasive Coligny, who was privately raising troops and money to aid of William of Orange.

The tension continued to increase in the miserable summer heat. The already crowded city began to fill with Protestants dressed in mourning black and Catholics from outside Paris. All had come for the wedding of the Huguenot prince and the Catholic princess. Paris had long been the center of the Catholic resistance to Protestantism. Parisians seethed as the Protestants filled up the hotels and camped in the alleys and side streets.

The wedding was scheduled for August 18, 1572. By midmorning the streets were impassable because of the throngs of people. The king's soldiers had to work to keep open an aisle for the bride and groom and their attendants. Shortly before noon, the procession, with the trumpeters in front, moved toward the church. Margo walked proudly, straight and tall despite the heat and the heavy violet velvet robe she wore. She later described herself that day: "I blazed in diamonds." The ceremony was an unusual mix of rites and rituals made necessary because neither the bride nor the groom would accept the other's religion.

That night, Coligny wrote to his wife that, although he realized he was in danger, he had to remain in Paris. He wrote of feeling "constrained to work to the utmost of [his] power" to advocate the war against Spain and to protect Henry and the other Huguenot leaders in the city.

The days after the wedding were filled with balls, banquets, and other entertainment. Coligny returned to the Louvre each day to participate in the celebrations. He also found time to meet with the ambassador from Protestant England to tell him that France would soon rid itself of the Roman Catholic Church.

On August 22, a Friday, Coligny left the palace around eleven in the morning to return to his hotel room. His walk took him past a house that had been occupied until two days before by the widow of the assassinated Duke of Guise. The duchess had mysteriously moved to much less comfortable quarters and left the house vacant. As Coligny walked past a musket shot rang out. Coligny was wounded in the arm; friends and bodyguards rushed him to his hotel.

There have been centuries of controversy over Catherine's role in the attempted assassination of Coligny. No one knows for certain if she had a hand in the conspiracy, although there is little doubt she wanted him dead. When the weapon was recovered it had a Guise family emblem carved into the stock. No one doubted the Guises were involved—the question has always been whether Catherine was the motivating force behind the attack.

The king was playing tennis when he learned of the attack. The always self-pitying Charles broke his racket in

disgust and cried out, "Am I never to be at peace?" Catherine held a quick meeting with her son Anjou before they rushed together to the king's side. At first, she tried to dissuade Charles from visiting the wounded Coligny. When he insisted, she demanded that she and Anjou be allowed to accompany him.

The royal party found Coligny in a heavily fortified room. Protestant soldiers stood outside his door and around his bed. Charles grasped Coligny's hand and promised to form a commission that would bring the assassins to justice. Coligny replied that a commission was not necessary. He suspected no one but Guise. If the king truly wanted justice he would arrest the duke. Catherine intervened and told Coligny to save his strength. He should not talk so much.

Catherine then had an extended meeting with Charles. She was in a dangerous predicament, especially if she had known of Guise's plan beforehand. If Guise was arrested he could implicate her in the plot. Even if she did not know of the plot, Coligny, who had such a hold over Charles, was still alive. Armed Protestant bands were already roaming the city demanding revenge. The Duke of Guise was quietly told to leave the city—but to not go too far.

Catherine asked Charles to convene an emergency Royal Council. It was held in a secluded corner of her favorite garden. At the meeting, an informant who had implanted himself in the Protestant leadership reported that there was a Huguenot conspiracy to take control of France. According to the spy, small bands of Huguenots were planning to enter

Opposite: The attempted assassination of the admiral de Coligny.

the Louvre in the evening on the following Tuesday. He claimed to have just left a meeting held around Coligny's bed. The king, his wife, and the rest of the royal family were to be seized and killed. Margo, Navarre, and his cousin Condé were also to be killed, clearing the path to the throne for Coligny, who would then declare France to be a Protestant kingdom.

Charles refused to believe that his beloved Coligny was planning his murder. He argued that the best course of action was to arrest Guise. That would show the Protestants that he was serious about capturing Coligny's attacker. If the duke wereto be tortured, he would tell them who else was behind the attack.

At this point Catherine played her trump card. What, she asked, if the king's mother was exposed as a conspirator? Would the king order her execution? Coligny was a traitor, she insisted, who wanted to destroy both her family and France in order to please his co-religionists in England and Geneva. The king had been blind to how Coligny threatened France, so she had taken the initiative to remove him herself. If Charles arrested Guise he would also have to arrest, and execute, the queen mother and her son, the Duke of Anjou.

Catherine then laid out the benefits of carrying out a swift, ruthless strike against the Huguenot leadership. Such a blow would cripple the movement, she said, and bring glory to the decisive French king. Charles could take no more. He interrupted her comments and yelled: "Kill the admiral [Coligny] if you wish; but you must also kill all the Huguenots, so that not one is left to reproach me. Kill them all! Kill them all! Kill them all." The king then fled the room.

7

Kill Them All

Charles had instantly gone from refusing to endorse the murder of Coligny to ordering the massacre of all the Huguenots. A list of Protestants to be killed was drawn up. Catherine later admitted to placing six names on it. She insisted that Henry of Navarre and his cousin Condé— both Princes of the Blood—be spared. She was afraid that wiping out the Bourbon family would leave her without protection from the ambitious Guises, who would be at the peak of their power once the Huguenot leadership was dead. Word was sent to Guise to slip quietly back into the city. He was about to be given the privilege of avenging his father's murder.

The order was sent out that the attack was to begin shortly before dawn the next day, Sunday, August 25, the day set aside to commemorate St. Bartholomew, the patron saint of healers. Catholics were warned to leave a light burning in the window to identify their houses.

Shortly after three in the morning, horsemen surrounded Coligny's hotel. His guards attempted to fight off the attackers but were quickly overwhelmed. Guise remained safely out on the street. When Coligny saw his killers approach his bed he demanded to be killed by a gentleman, as his rank entitled, but his request was ignored. Stabbed seven times, his body was tossed out the window. Guise confirmed his identity. Later he was beheaded and hung for public display by his feet. A horse's tail was placed where his head once was.

Coligny's murder was the signal for a wholesale slaughter to begin. It quickly jumped out of Guise's control. Hundreds of Protestants were murdered. Fetuses were taken out of the bodies of pregnant women and smashed to a pulp. One man bragged that he had personally beheaded four hundred Protestants in only eight hours.

The savagery inevitably became more general. Catholics took advantage of the chaos to kill Catholic enemies; old scores were settled. One publisher removed his chief business rival by roasting him over a bonfire fueled by his own books. Bankers, pawnbrokers, and landlords were killed. Husbands killed wives. The stench of blood and vacated bodies filled the hot, steamy city.

The rampage spread from Paris into the countryside and other towns and cities. The killing lasted until it ran out of victims on the afternoon of August 26. The actual number of dead is unknown. While estimates have run as high as one hundred thousand, most historians place the number closer to ten thousand, with approximately half of them in Paris.

On Tuesday August 26, the day Catherine's spy had claimed the Huguenots had planned to seize power, the king led a procession to the Palace of Justice, where thanks was given that the Huguenot plot had been foiled. It was noted that the queen mother seemed to be in particularly high spirits. She later wrote to Philip II of Spain and asked him to share in her joy that her son had enjoyed such great success against their common enemy. It was said that after reading the letter, Philip smiled and laughed out loud in public for the first and only time.

More laughter was heard in Paris when Henry of Navarre kneeled and accepted communion. He had been told to convert or die. After his first Catholic service, Catherine turned to the bench that held the foreign ambassadors and broke out in a joyful laugh. Apparently, she was convinced that the conversion of Henry and the slaughter of the Huguenot leaders had ended the religious conflict in France once and for all.

When he learned of the St. Bartholomew Day Massacre, a jubilant Pope Gregory XIII held a mass to rejoice at the victory over the heretics. He had a commemorative medal minted in celebration, and thanked Catherine for the bold move.

The reaction elsewhere was more negative. Thousands of pamphlets poured into France proclaiming that Charles was an irresponsible tyrant and that French citizens had an obligation to take up arms against tyranny. The pamphlets disparaged Catherine as a foreigner, an Italian nonetheless, who had lost all credibility because of her deceptions.

Although Queen Elizabeth of England's response was muted, she let it be known that she did not trust Catherine. This was a setback because Catherine was trying to arrange the marriage of her youngest son, Hercule, the Duke of Alençon, to that Protestant queen. In the end, this plan would fail, and

Hercule, the Duke of Alençon.

Elizabeth would never marry. Publicly, Catherine claimed the massacre was an act of self-defense made necessary by an uncovered Huguenot plot, but few on either side believed that. It would have been a relatively simple matter to arrest the leaders of the plot. They preferred to see her as a student of Machiavelli, the writer who advised government leaders to commit all atrocities necessary to prevent any possible conciliation or negotiation in times of conflict. Catherine's actions seemed to follow his advice: "One [a leader] must color his conduct, and be a great dissembler; and men are so simple, so absorbed in present necessities, that they are easily deceived."

But it soon became apparent that any hopes that the massacre would end the religious wars, or bring peace to

Opposite: The St. Bartholomew's Day Massacre, painted by François Dubais, a Protestant who survived the attack. (*Musée Cantonal des Beaux-Arts, Lausanne.*)

France, were misguided. Within days, another Huguenot rebellion, the fourth, began when Huguenot forces seized the port city of La Rochelle. This was dangerous to France because now the English had an easy way to ship soldiers and supplies into France if Elizabeth decided to back the Protestants. The city had to be retaken.

Catherine's favorite son, Henry, Duke of Anjou, had gained a name as a military hero against the Protestants. Now she sent him out to retake La Rochelle. But this time he went without Marshal of Tavannes, who had been the real leader of the royal forces in the earlier victories. Although his men heavily outnumbered the Protestant troops holding the harbor city, Anjou was unable to drive them out. What had started as a grand military escapade quickly became a miserable siege that threatened to go on indefinitely.

Catherine had plans for Anjou. The childless king of Poland was mortally ill. His replacement would be elected by a council of nobility whom Catherine had taken pains to bribe. When word came that the Polish king had died, she had Charles arrange a quick peace with the Protestants in La Rochelle and had Anjou hurry home to Paris. The Polish nobles did as they had promised, and Anjou was now the king of Poland. After his coronation in Cracow, in 1572, Catherine wrote to her favorite son: "I hardly know how to thank God, for now I see you in the role I have always wanted for you." It was not a job he wanted. Poland was a barbaric and cold place far away from Paris. But Catherine assured him it was temporary. It was obvious to everyone that Charles's health was failing. When he died, Anjou could

This tapestry, woven to commemorate the arrival of the Polish ambassadors to offer the crown of Poland to Henry of Anjou, shows the marked opulence of the Valois court. Catherine is pictured in black at the center of the scene. *(Louvre, Paris)*

leave Poland and assume his rightful place on the French throne.

Sending Anjou to far off Poland was a risk, however. The Politiques, an increasingly powerful group of moderate Catholics, had been shocked and angered by the St. Bartholomew Day Massacre. They had not trusted Catherine or Anjou before the sudden attack, and now that, combined with Catherine's secret collaboration with the hated Guise, meant the Politiques were not ready to automatically support Anjou. They sent word to Alençon that they would consider putting him on the throne when Charles died if he would back their cause. He agreed.

After Anjou left for Poland, the Politiques met in southern France to plan how to put Alençon on the throne. They would have preferred Louis de Condé or Henry of Navarre to take the throne—these practical men were under no illusion that Alençon would make a strong and trustworthy king—but both were still virtual prisoners of the court. They had even marched with Anjou to recapture La Rochelle. The Politiques would settle for Alençon to be their puppet, if it would end the religious conflict and unite France. They planned to issue an edict of religious toleration once they were in power.

The Politiques tried to keep their scheme secret but, inevitably, Catherine learned of it and had her son Alençon imprisoned. When she heard that her astrologer had been working with Alençon and conjuring evil spells against the crown, she had him imprisoned too. But the imprisonment only raised Alençon's status with the Politiques.

Charles ate and drank little, and grew weaker and weaker. An English ambassador reported: "The King is reduced to skin and bones, his legs and thighs are so weak that he cannot hold himself up." With Anjou in Poland, Alençon in prison, and Charles preoccupied by death, fifty-five-year-old Catherine once again resorted to scheming to retain her authority. She wrote letters to leaders in France and England and reported that Charles was feeling better. She said she gave thanks to God for sparing him and hoped for a complete recovery soon. Those who worked in Charles's court knew that there was no truth to these statements. Charles himself knew that his death was near and affirmed that Catherine would act as his regent until Anjou returned from Poland. Twenty-four-year-old Charles died on May 30, 1574.

For the fourth time, Catherine had seen a king of France die. Two of them had been her sons, one her husband. She informed Anjou in Poland that his brother was dead and that now he was King Henry III. It was a trying time. She was grieving for her son Charles and anxiously awaiting the return of Anjou. There was always the chance the Politiques would kidnap her and release Alençon from jail to crown him king.

For forty days the king's body lay in a metal casket. Twelve members of four major religious orders prayed for him day and night. In the adjoining room an effigy of Charles sat on a throne, clothed in satin, ermine, and a jeweled crown. At Charles's funeral, first came cries of "The King is dead," and immediately after came the cries, "The King lives. Long live Henry III!"

8

No Peace

Until Anjou returned, Catherine was in control of the country as regent. She had imprisoned Alençon, who might otherwise have raised a claim to the crown. Now she imprisoned Francis de Montmorency, a leader of the Politiques. She told the Estates General that she wielded the authority of the throne because her son had asked her to do so until he returned from Poland. Full of energy, Catherine overworked her secretaries and exhausted her servants.

Catherine waited impatiently for Henry III to return from Poland. He did not share in her sense of urgency. Instead, he stopped at many cities along the way. He took a detour through Italy, where he fully enjoyed the social life in Venice and Milan. As he dallied, Catherine was busy writing up instructions on how to rule. He must be diligent, pay personal attention to all matters, be fiscally prudent, and speak with authority and dignity. He should get up early each morning to prepare for the work of the day. He must never let petitioners speak to his aides; they must learn that he alone was in charge of dispensing favors. She specified that he must carry out government reforms immediately, saying that she would have done so herself but she did not have the authority. She wrote that he should be judicious and calm about his new responsibilities: "I am sure that there has never been a king as wise as you."

Two and a half months after Catherine had summoned him, Anjou arrived in France. He wore a violet satin tunic and cape and dangling earrings and bracelets of coral and silver. Violet and red ribbons decorated all of his clothes. Assuming the throne as King Henry III, he reduced the number of members of the Royal Council and restricted access to himself. He made a poor impression on the court, which soon rejected him personally as well as politically. Catherine refused to see what members of the court were telling her—Henry III had never grown up. During his coronation, on February 13, 1575, he was heard to complain that his crown was too heavy and that it hurt his head. He still played children's games. But Catherine would not admit, at least publicly, that her favorite son was a disappointment to her and the people of France.

Henry III made it clear that he would make decisions on his own and in secret. He did not intend to grant any concessions to the Huguenots, reduce taxes, or convene the Estates General. He would personally rid France of all her enemies by whatever force was necessary. He managed the

Henry III in a costume typical of his elaborate taste. *(Musée Condé, Chantilly)*

seemingly impossible feat of forcing the Huguenots and the moderate Catholics to form a secret alliance against him.

A few days after the coronation ceremony, Henry married Louise de Vaudémont—against Catherine's wishes. Catherine saw no political benefit from this marriage but could not convince her son to change his mind. This was just one of many times that Henry III defied his mother. She told him to be warm and open; he withdrew from the nobles and declared his offices off limits to them. She told him to respect those who helped him; he demanded that they bow before him. She told him not to play favorites among his courtiers; he gathered around him a group of young, high-spirited men on whom he lavished gifts. She told him to practice tolerance; he refused to even see Huguenot delegates. By November 1574, four armies were in open conflict in France. Henry III commanded one of these armies himself.

Alençon escaped from imprisonment and joined the revolt against his brother. With his sister Margo's support, he proclaimed himself Governor-General and Defender of the Liberties of France. Alençon did not seem to be making overt preparations for war, but Catherine knew of his unquenched ambition to rule. As heir apparent to the throne, he now insisted on being called Monsieur. He even attempted to bring Henry of Navarre in on a scheme to assassinate the king, but Henry was too wily to be drawn into the plot.

Alençon and his supporters sent many petitions to Henry III seeking religious and political reform. When the new king did not respond, Alençon issued a manifesto: "We have decided to win by force the peace and tranquillity that we could not achieve by reason." This manifesto apparently convinced Henry III that he needed to seek peace. He asked Catherine to negotiate with Alençon for him.

Catherine said, "I will go myself and bring back the wretched boy [Alençon] wherever he may be." To persuade Alençon to settle peacefully, she awarded him the provinces of Berry, Touraine, and Anjou, along with a generous annual income. They negotiated a treaty called the Peace of Monsieur under which Huguenots were allowed to worship anywhere in the country except within two leagues of Paris or the royal court, wherever it might be located. Protestants could build churches and hospitals, gain admission to schools and all professions, and seek justice in a bipartisan court. Both Louis de Condé and Henry of Navarre were made governors of Huguenot territories.

Catherine did not want to make the settlement because she knew it would enrage the Guises and other militant Catholics. But she felt she had no other options. She believed that Alençon already had the power to seize the throne. An illusion of a royal victory was better than the alternative. The lessons she had learned as a daughter of the Medicis and a student of Machiavelli was that appearances were often more important that reality.

Huguenots complained that Alençon had acted only in his own interest by signing the treaty and returning to the royal family fold. Catholics complained that Catherine had sold them out. In reaction to the Peace of Monsieur, the

Duke of Guise created the Catholic League, an organization dedicated to the eradication of heresy. All Catholics were invited to join the League and to take up arms. Soon the Catholic League controlled the Estates General. A Catholic commander of royal troops refused to let Louis de Condé even enter the territory he had been granted in the treaty.

After all her years of struggle, everything seemed to be collapsing in on Catherine. In response to the formation of the Catholic League, Huguenot leaders began to recruit reinforcements and German mercenaries came to France to join them. Within a year, Alençon, who had again thrown in with the Politiques and the Huguenots, had an army of 30,000 soldiers under his command. King Henry III, meanwhile, refused to attend to the business of state, or to listen to Catherine's advice. Dressed in satin and beribboned clothes, he joined groups of pilgrims who toured the streets flagellating each other and singing psalms.

Catherine tried desperately to create the illusion that Henry was ruling well. It was an impossible task, even for the wily queen mother. Henry insisted on filling the palace with cages of chattering monkeys and multicolored parrots; tiny dogs ran everywhere. His hands flashed with jewels and his ears hung with heavy earrings. Catherine told him that his subjects were complaining that he was a homosexual, which would make him an unacceptable ruler in the eyes of the Catholic Church. She could not make him understand that by his generous gestures to his *mignons,* his favorites at court, he was taking money from his subjects who lacked food, clothing, and shelter. Furthermore, he was unwilling

Henry's court was characterized by eccentric behavior and extravagant parties.

to even attempt to reconcile the Guise party and the Catholic League to the provisions of the Peace of Monsieur.

Catherine wrote letters to political and religious opponents begging them to help her son who, she said, was working for peace. But neither Protestants nor Catholics trusted Catherine.

Aging and worn down from the strain of propping up her son, Catherine was devastated by the death of her daughter Claude. Of her three remaining children, Margo and Alençon had forfeited her trust and the once-beloved Henry considered her a nuisance.

In December 1576, the Estates General was convened at Blois, a magnificent Gothic building with a solid royal background in the history of France. To everyone's surprise Henry gave a good speech about the glorious history of the country under his father and grandfather. He said he would prefer death to a divided kingdom and gave public thanks to Catherine for her guidance of the country through difficult times. Although they were startled at this change in their king, the delegates did not trust him. They had seen the indolence, the lavish entertainments while his duties went undone, his wasteful spending of public money, and his favoritism. They refused to provide the revenues he asked for.

As afraid as she was about the German mercenaries she remembered from her childhood and the horrible sack of Rome, Catherine knew that the threat of the Guise family and the Catholic League was more dangerous than the threat of the Huguenots. The Guises had a strong military organization. The Duke of Guise let it be known that he was willing to free France from its present rulers, outlaw the Huguenots, imprison Alençon, and exile Henry and Catherine.

Finally, Henry realized the danger posed by both the Catholic League and the Huguenots. He placed himself at the head of the Catholic League and sent out orders to recruit soldiers for a war against Protestant heresy. This war dragged on through the summer of 1577, when the Huguenots decided that it was best to sue for peace. In September, the Peace of Bergerac, sometimes called the King's Peace, was established. Essentially it conceded the right of the Huguenots to live in peace in France but it restricted their right to worship. Neither side was satisfied with the treaty.

Catherine continued to hold out for a policy of tolerance. She was frustrated that, as she put it, Henry "disapproves of everything I do. . . . clearly I am not free to do as I wish." Still she tried to influence members of the court, the Catholic League, and Huguenots. Against Henry's will, she told the Estates General that she would not allow Catholics to destroy France.

The French treasury was nearly empty. In vain, Catherine appealed to Henry: "I beg you to control your finances very carefully in order to raise money for your service without having to rob your people, for you are on the brink of a general revolt—and whoever tells you otherwise deceives you." Henry continued to spend recklessly. When he could no longer obtain money from already over-taxed subjects or from the church, he sold royal offices to the highest bidders.

Catherine as an older woman.

Sixty-year-old Catherine was now extremely stout and suffered from rheumatism. Nevertheless, she decided to travel through the country to encourage people to practice religious tolerance and to remain loyal to their king. During the summer of 1578 she traveled for hours each day, sometimes riding a mule over rough roads. There was a drought that summer, cattle were dying in the fields, crops dried up, and famine and the plague were widespread.

There was also a secret purpose to her trip. Henry of Navarre had managed to escape from confinement in 1576— he slipped away while boar hunting with the Duke of Guise—and had returned to Navarre. Margo was left behind, but he vowed to return for her one day. As soon as he was safely home, Henry returned to the Protestant faith.

Henry and Margo were never in love, although he was known to become jealous when he heard stories of the lovers she took. But the events surrounding their wedding had created a bond between them. Margo had probably saved his life the night Coligny was killed by hiding him in the castle. She had convinced him to convert to Catholicism. She had also drawn him and her younger brother together. Alençon now considered Navarre his best friend. They shared a deep hatred and distrust of King Henry III. It was Navarre who encouraged Alençon to leave Paris and to join with the Huguenots and the Politiques.

Margo and Navarre were both wily and intelligent political operators. Although he was Protestant and she Catholic, both were relatively moderate in their religion. They would later divorce, but for the present they were held together by a mutual respect and a commitment to moderate, secular politics over religious enthusiasm.

Catherine received permission from Henry III to take

Margo, her brother Alençon, and her husband, Henry of Navarre. *(Uffizi, Florence)*

Margo with her on her trip. Catherine had begun to realize that, although she still deeply loved her son, he was a disappointment as a king. Alençon was even worse, in her estimation. He had led a revolt when only twenty, and had managed to force concessions in the Peace of Monsieur, but he was even more unstable than Henry. The king was childless, and it seemed likely he would die without leaving an heir.

Catherine was beginning to realize that the future of France was Henry of Navarre. He was next in line after Alençon. Although she could probably control Alençon, she knew Navarre would be the better king. But she needed to find a way to get in his good graces, to exert some control over him, in case he became king. What better way than to return his wife to him?

She wrote to Navarre: "Come to dine or stay the night whichever you please, just so long as I have an hour to talk with you . . . and put an end to all these comings and goings." Their first meetings went well. Both rulers declared they wanted peace, and both deplored the civil war. They decided to meet again in a few months. Catherine and Margo resumed their tour of eastern France.

During the trip, which took place mostly in the winter months, Catherine set herself a strict schedule of public functions, private interviews, and evenings of dictating accounts of her travels to secretaries who sent them on to the king. She did not let the pain of arthritis, bouts of colic, or attacks of gout distract her. Her body was deteriorating, but her energy and determination remained strong. Henry III, however, did not respond to a single communication, even the ones asking for his suggestions and opinions. As mothers have for centuries, Catherine blamed his behavior on his companions.

In February 1579, Catherine, Margo, and Henry of

Navarre met for twenty-four days in Nérac, the capital city of Navarre. There were pageants and public ceremonies; Queen Margo was welcomed for the first time to Navarre and impressed everyone with her dignity, intelligence, and grace.

When the real work between Catherine and Navarre began, she and her deputies worked ceaselessly. They focused on politics and economics, not religion. Catherine tried to not favor either Huguenots or Catholics. She was desperate for an immediate peace before France was destroyed, and she was willing to make some concessions. Despite the cold and damp, and her poor health, Catherine kept an even temper except once when delegates tried to walk out. She exploded in fury and told them that if they did not cooperate, she would have them hanged as rebels. They came back to the table.

In the final agreement, the Articles of Nérac, both sides agreed to commit themselves to peace. Catherine wrote to Henry III that she thought the terms could end the religious conflict. In reality, little had changed. The Catholic League was committed to keeping the Huguenot Navarre from the throne and the Huguenots would never trust the person they held most responsible for the St. Bartholomew's Day Massacre. Nevertheless, an optimistic Catherine said goodbye to her daughter and headed back to Paris with the agreement in hand.

9
A Race for the Throne

After the meetings with Navarre, before she returned to Paris, Catherine traveled to towns in the south of France to assure them the king was concerned for their well-being. What she discovered during this tour was that the religious conflict in France was still very much alive. In a few places, Catherine was able to persuade the ruling councils of villages to admit representatives from both the Catholic and Huguenot sides, but her victories were small and the trip took her much longer than she had expected.

Catherine, exhausted and discouraged, finally returned to Paris in November 1579, only to discover the city seemed to be on the verge of insurrection. Henry had done nothing to ease the tensions there. All of his time was given to spending money he did not have, reading poetry with a club he had formed, and going to parties with his friends. While in the south, Catherine had been able to persuade several Huguenot communities to lay down their arms in exchange for her promise that the king would pay attention to their grievances, but she was unable to get her son to carry through on her promises. He was still under the influence of the Duke of Guise and the Catholic League, which had grown into the most powerful political force in Paris. Guise told the king never to negotiate with heretics. The only solution was for them to convert or die.

Catherine, now almost seventy, was physically and emotionally exhausted. She suffered from gout and worsening rheumatism. A once hearty eater, she had lost her appetite. But there was to be no rest for her. Alençon had left Paris again and was in the Netherlands leading Huguenot troops against Spain. "I cannot believe that you want to ruin this kingdom [the Netherlands] as well as your own—and this is what it will mean if war breaks out again," she wrote to her youngest son. Her letter had no effect. Alençon dreamed only of attaining glory as a political and military leader.

The economy was a disaster. Men paid bribes to acquire government jobs, and taxes were extremely high. Members of the royal court fought among themselves and did little to control corruption. An epidemic of contagious whooping cough struck Paris. Hundreds of children and adults died.

King Henry III continued to scandalize all of France. He surrounded himself with delicate young boys, his *mignons,* and gyrated between open debauchery and religious fanaticism. During the religious phases he led the *mignons,* who had replaced their purple and satin silk

clothes with the drab robes of religious penitents, in parades through the streets of Paris. Sometimes Henry would crawl for miles as the *mignons* followed behind flagellating themselves with whips. The citizens of Paris would jeer and laugh from their windows at the crawling king. Over time the king's health began to deteriorate and he became subject to delusions.

Despite dozens of baths, potions, and prayers, Henry's wife Queen Louise had not borne a child. Eventually, even Catherine admitted she was not likely to ever do so. If Henry died, the only man standing between the throne and Navarre would be Alençon.

Guise and the Catholic League ignored the agreement Catherine had hammered out with Navarre. Their attacks on Protestant villages grew increasingly horrible. In one incident Guise fighters came upon four teenage Protestant girls on the road. After raping them repeatedly they stuffed gunpowder into their bodies, lighted them, and cheered while the screaming girls exploded.

These stories and others soon reached Navarre. He had come to an agreement with Catherine because he knew it was only a matter of time before he became king. He expected Guise to try to stand in his way, but was willing to be patient and to prepare for that fight when it came. Now he had no choice but to go to war again. Many Huguenots distrusted him not only for his earlier willingness to convert to avoid execution, but also because of his Catholic wife. Not to revenge the attacks by the Catholic League would put

Opposite: One of Henry's *mignons*.

This engraving depicts the battle between the Huguenots and the Catholics at Cahors.

his position as leader of the Protestants at risk. In April 1580, open religious war broke out.

During this war, Henry of Navarre began to display the talent, courage, and intelligence that would eventually make him one of France's greatest kings. He had limited men and money. He selected a Catholic city, Cahors, and, after careful planning, made a surprise twilight attack. Within hours he had seized the city. King Henry III had no choice but to send troops to try to retake Cahors. Navarre, having made his point, left the city and returned to the safety of Nécar. The war dragged on; innocent people on both sides were murdered, raped, and brutalized in various ways.

Catherine, old and sick, despaired at how her adopted but beloved country was suffering. Her children continued to be an embarrassment. Henry began to grant his favorites among the *mignons* titles of nobility. When three of them were fatally wounded in a duel with followers of the Duke of Guise, Henry offered one hundred thousand pieces of gold to any doctor who could save their lives.

Meanwhile, Margo returned to Paris from Navarre. She had grown bored in the country and had been embarrassed by her husband's latest affair. She moved into a house near the Louvre that was soon notorious for the parties that occurred there. One ambassador even referred to it as a bordello. When her brother, the king, chastised her for bringing shame on the family at an official banquet, the angry Margo returned to Navarre the very next day.

Catherine again tried to arrange a marriage between Queen Elizabeth of England and Alençon. She even sent a

The Spanish Netherlands city of Antwerp.

minister to London to work out the details. But it soon became clear that Elizabeth had no intention of marrying the ugly Catholic prince who was half her age. Embarrassed and embittered at the public rejection, Alençon returned to his private army and attacked the city of Antwerp in the Netherlands in February 1582. When the citizens convinced him they were ready to surrender and asked him to lead his troops in a victory parade through the city streets, Alençon was more than happy to agree. Once he and his men were safely within city walls though, the gates were closed behind them and a combined force of professional soldiers and armed citizens killed at least twelve thousand of his men.

Alençon managed to escape Antwerp and flee to Paris. There he threw himself at his brother Henry's feet and begged forgiveness. Henry embraced him and said that he would give him the succession of the kingdom. Catherine cried with happiness at the reconciliation. She wrote, "Believe me, I am going to die very happy." A month later, Alençon began to bleed from the nose and mouth. He became emaciated and was eventually too weak to stand. He was dead by June.

Catherine mourned the loss of yet another child, but there was a sigh of relief from most of France. They had suffered through the years of being ruled by Catherine's children. The question that hung in the air, and promised to create even more misery, was which family would next control the throne—Bourbon (Navarre) or Guise.

By law, Henry of Navarre, who alone could trace his ancestry back to Hugh Capet, the founder of the French monarchy, was the lawful successor to the throne. But he was Protestant, and the ambitious Duke of Guise was determined Navarre would never become king. Catherine's solution was to try to convince Navarre to once again convert to Catholicism. She had been trying to achieve this for years but Navarre had categorically stated that he would not. Catherine developed a three-part plan. First, Navarre would convert and claim the throne. Second, Margo would become queen of France and bear a male heir. Third, Catherine as mother of the late king and current queen would once again have a hand in ruling France.

But Navarre refused to convert, so King Henry talked of divorcing his wife Louise and marrying someone else to redouble his efforts to produce an heir. Because no one thought it was his wife's fault he had no child, this became the subject of countless jokes at court and in the streets of Paris.

The Duke of Guise rushed to take advantage of the ever-weakening throne and Navarre's refusal to convert. He incited the Catholic League, reinvigorated by Alençon's death and Henry's failing health, to be ready for action. If the Protestant Navarre became king, he told his troops, Catholicism would be outlawed in France. He told them horror stories of how Catholics were persecuted in England and other Protestant countries.

The Guises intensified their military operations. It was as though Alençon's death was the signal to start the race for the throne. Philip II of Spain agreed to finance them. They used the Spanish money to hire six thousand Swiss troops and mercenaries from Germany, built up stocks of weapons, and began leading uprisings throughout France. The king's neglect had left the country open for rebellion. The Duke of Guise claimed he no longer had aspirations to the throne. Instead, he endorsed sixty-three-year-old Charles, cardinal of Lorraine, who had a legitimate claim to the throne because he was a Prince of the Blood—although his claim was not as strong as Navarre's.

King Henry III busied himself with setting up what he called rules to reform the Royal Council. One of his new rules was that members would wear garments of violet velvet from October to May and garments of violet satin for the summer months. He also imposed rules for actions such as handing him a drink of water. These "reforms" lost him even more support among the nobility. Justice was poorly administered, soldiers pillaged towns and villages, and taxes were higher than ever. The price of bread had doubled since 1578. Henry dealt with the problems by issuing an Edict of Union, declaring that all leagues and associations that threatened the throne were guilty of treason and would be punished appropriately. But, as everyone knew when it was announced, he was unable to enforce the edict. Issuing it had only highlighted his political weakness.

At a secret meeting the Duke of Guise signed a treaty with Spain "for the conservation of the Catholic religion and the extirpation of all sects and heresies in France and the Low Countries." Spain agreed to support the cardinal of Bourbon as the next king of France.

Henry III learned of the supposedly secret meeting. Like a frightened child, he turned to his mother. He begged her to make a compromise with the Guises. Once again, Catherine was asked to accomplish the impossible. Although she still had not recovered from the gout and suffered with a persistent cough and pains in her side and thigh, she asked to be taken to meet the Duke of Guise.

Catherine was confined to her bed during her meeting with Guise. She had a secretary keep careful notes of all proceedings. The duke praised Henry for banning the Protestant religion in France but said that more needed to be done. He wanted to root out all Protestants whether they were worshiping publicly or not. Representatives of the Catholic League accompanied Guise to the meeting, insisting that all their demands must be met. They were not willing to compromise. When the bargaining was over, Catherine reluctantly signed an agreement that required all French subjects to profess to be Catholics and to take communion within the next six months or be exiled. Control of the military was given to the Duke of Guise. The agreement was a personal and public humiliation for Catherine. She feared for the fate of France.

Catherine begged King Henry to prepare for war. There was no chance Navarre and the Huguenots would convert or leave. But Henry refused to prepare. Instead, he took his frustration out on her. She should have never signed the agreement. Next he turned his wrath on the pope, who reacted by expelling the French ambassador to the Vatican.

King Henry III retreated into solitary fasting and prayer. One of his aides commented, "One can hardly get the king out of a monk's cell." A messenger reported that Henry "had a sword by his side, a hood upon his shoulders, a little bonnet upon his head, a basket full of small dogs hung around his neck by a large ribbon; and he held himself so still that in speaking to us he neither moved head nor feet nor hands."

Catherine was devastated when Margo, who had fallen out with her husband Navarre, joined the Catholic League that sought to overthrow her brother. Catherine wrote: "I realize that God has given me this creature [Margo] for the punishment of my sins." She convinced Henry to send soldiers to seize Margo, who spent the next fourteen years in Auvergne, an area in the center of France, with no contact from any member of her family.

Catherine and the king realized they had only one place to turn. Henry of Navarre agreed to meet with them and the Royal Council as long as the meeting was held in Huguenot territory. They assembled in the small town of St. Brice. Fifty Catholics loyal to the king and fifty Huguenots guarded the house, all fully armed. Navarre and Catherine met for the first time in six years. Catherine was swollen from gout. The ruff around her neck fit tightly over her chins. She walked with difficulty on swollen legs. But she still had energy. Catherine warned Navarre that he would regret it all his life if he did not accept the peace she offered now. If he converted, the war would end and he would have a clear path to the throne. But Navarre knew he could not convert until the current king was dead. Converting prematurely would leave him at the mercy of the Catholics because his Huguenot supporters would certainly desert him. Navarre had learned the hard way that he needed to look out for his own interests. He was not about to trust Catherine with his life.

10

Choosing a New King

After a fifty-year struggle to keep her family on the throne and save France from sectarian strife, Catherine was finally defeated. Despite decades of maneuvering, she was where she had been before the St. Bartholomew's Day Massacre—caught between the Duke of Guise and the king of Navarre. All Catherine could say was "God must be very angry and we very wicked people that we must suffer such great evils with no hope of escaping them unless He himself turn His hand to our help."

Catherine left Navarre and returned to the Louvre where she was so stricken with gout that she could barely get out of bed. Still, when Henry III insisted that she travel to Reims to fashion a compromise with the Catholic League, she made the trip. At Reims, she told the Duke of Guise that the king would be pleased to work with him and the Catholic

League for the good of the country. She made wild promises and exaggerated the king's authority. Guise was not fooled. He knew that the king and his mother were virtually powerless.

Catherine noted that comets had appeared four times between 1577 and 1586, an unusually high frequency. In the Hôtel de la Reine in Paris, she had a tall Doric column built. Inside the column was a staircase leading to a platform observatory. Legend says that Catherine had it built for her astrologers. Some astrologers had predicted that 1588 would be a year with many strange incidents including, perhaps, the end of the world. As early as January of that year, it seemed that the astrologers were correct—flood, famine, and cold struck France. On one unforgettable day, unusually dense fog covered the city, turning day into night. The fog, like the flood and famine, was interpreted by many as a sign of great changes to come.

In May 1588, the Duke of Guise entered the city gates. As he traveled through the city, thirty thousand supporters fell in behind him. Catherine was brought out on a litter to meet him. She looked short and heavy on the litter, dressed in black as she had been since the death of her husband so many years before. The duke sat tall and straight on his horse, handsome in white satin with a black velvet cloak. As he approached, Catherine heard the crowd cheer: "Long live the Duke of Guise!"

Catherine welcomed him coldly. Later the king joined them and they meet for three hours. Each talked past the other, refusing to respond to the other's comments—compromise did not seem possible here, either.

This painting by François Brunel depicts the procession of the Catholic League to the Place de Grève in Paris. *(Musée Carnavalet, Paris.)*

Around the Sorbonne University, students gathered to show their resistance to Henry. They put up a barricade of rocks, cobblestones, barrels, and old pieces of wood. The news of this first barricade traveled quickly. Soon, throughout the city, dozens of barricades, designed to keep royal soldiers out of the neighborhoods, were thrown up. What became known as the Day of Barricades signaled the beginning of intense rioting against the king.

In desperation, Henry and Catherine appealed to the Duke of Guise to intervene to stop the demonstrations. The duke rode through the streets and quieted the crowds with a few simple words. The king's troops were allowed to carry their dead and wounded back to the Louvre. Once more Catherine was brought out to meet with the duke. The citizens on the street crowded around her. Many reached out to jostle her and yelled out the old complaints and insults she had heard when she first rode through the streets of Marseilles as a girl of fourteen. They still considered her to be a foreigner. The heavily Catholic crowd resented her for compromising with the Huguenots. They called her a Jezebel. Her trip through the streets was slow, partly because of her weight and fragility, partly because of the teeming crowds.

In the meeting, Catherine tried to bargain with the duke. He demanded to be appointed Lieutenant General of France and that Henry of Navarre be excluded from the royal succession. All enemies of the Catholic League were to be removed from public office, and all important government posts were to be given to faithful Catholics. The king could keep his title, but would retain no authority.

Catherine went back to the Louvre to discuss the conditions with Henry. Neither Henry nor his ministers wanted to accept the treaty. They asked Catherine to meet with the duke again. During that next meeting, a messenger broke into their room with the news that the king had fled Paris. The duke accused Catherine of keeping him distracted while her son sneaked out of town. Catherine denied the charge, but she could not explain why Henry had fled.

Catherine received a note from Henry, who was in Chartres, a city about forty-five miles southwest of Paris. He ordered her to stay in Paris and to continue negotiations with the duke. Catherine sent out the word that Henry had not fled, but simply could not stay in Paris because of the mobs that had been incited to riot by Guise. She told the Council that her son was continuing to carry out the tasks of government. As usual, she made up a story for every question asked of her, trying desperately to salvage the reputation of the crown and her family.

From Chartres, Henry sent word that he would agree to

The city of Chartres, where Henry hid out during the Catholic League's demonstrations.

appoint Guise Lieutenant General of France in return for a guarantee of his own safety in Paris. Guise refused to grant him safety. Catherine continued doggedly in the negotiations, but there was no chance of making an impact on the other side. For six weeks after Henry fled, she spent hours writing letters and contacting people, begging them for help.

The Duke of Guise reentered Paris triumphantly amid cheers. Those few loyal to Henry begged him to return or, if he would not, to appoint the queen mother as his mediator. Then, as suddenly as he had left, King Henry did return and announced he would yield to any demands from the duke. In vain, Catherine begged him to stand strong. Did he not see that he was humiliating her and speaking against the best interests of the country?

Henry fired his eight principal advisors, all of whom had been recommended by Catherine, and appointed new men, mostly *mignons,* who had no obvious qualifications for the job. He declared that he wanted to handle the affairs of state by himself. Catherine could do nothing.

The Duke of Guise believed it was time to convene an Estates General. He planned to convince the nobility that he and his aides were the rulers of France. The cardinal of Bourbon would be the king, but the real power would reside with the Catholic League. Guise arranged to have the Estates General packed with his supporters and members of the League. The meeting opened on October 16, 1588 with the Duke of Guise, splendidly dressed in white satin, leading the king to a place on the raised platform between his mother and his wife. Henry began the meeting with a speech praising his own work on behalf of the kingdom. He went on to praise the Edict of Union by which he had declared that he would root out any person or association which might try to raise money or troops to overcome the crown. He said he would be kind enough to excuse those of his subjects who had persisted in such actions in the past but that henceforth they would be severely punished for any hint of treason. The representatives paid little attention to his bombast. Instead they showered him with questions about high taxes, royal extravagance, and his neglect of his royal duties. Henry was trapped. He had no choice but to agree to many concessions, including lowering taxes, stopping his methods of raising money by selling jobs in the court, and asserting that he would more vigorously root out heresy.

Catherine became ill with cold, cough, and fever and could scarcely get out of bed. Messengers brought her rumors of impending violence. On December 20, Henry met secretly with his most trusted assistants to decide what to do about the Duke of Guise. This group decided that Henry would first accuse him of treason and then challenge him to a duel. Accordingly, they invited the duke to meet with them. Although he feared a trap, the duke did not dare to refuse the invitation—to do so might imply that Henry was the stronger man.

The fears of Guise's supporters were confirmed. He was assassinated even before he reached the room where Henry was supposedly awaiting him. Hearing the commotion, the cardinal of Lorraine rushed to his brother's aid. Henry had him killed also. Afterward, Henry went upstairs to his mother and told her that he had assassinated the duke. One legend says that he bragged to her that he was now indisputably the king of France.

The news of the two murders spread quickly around the city. Parisians went wild with anger and grief. They looted the royal apartments at the Louvre, and threw pictures and statues of the king into the Seine. They demanded revenge.

This was the last straw for Catherine. Although she had no love for the duke, she could not accept Henry's execution of Lorraine. The cardinal was a man of God, and Catherine wondered how God would ever pardon her son for killing him. It was reported that Catherine spoke to a friar about her son: "Oh, wretched man! What has he done? . . . I am afraid he may lose his body, soul, and kingdom." She was sure that Guise's supporters would avenge the duke's death. She could not convince her son to take precautions for his own safety; Henry believed the assassination had solved

In this scene by Paul Delaroche, Henry is surrounded by his court after the fatal stabbing of the Duke of Guise. *(Courtesy of Art Resource.)*

most of his political problems. To solve the rest, he imprisoned the leaders of the Catholic League. These acts alienated any support he might have received from the papacy.

Catherine saw little of Henry in the week between Christmas and New Year's Day. She did visit the cardinal of Bourbon, whom Henry had also imprisoned. She wanted to apologize to him for her son's actions but he refused to listen to her. He blamed her for the chaos and devastation in France. He told her, "You will be the death of us all."

This rejection affected Catherine physically and emotionally. She lay in bed for three days suffering from chills and fever as well as from rheumatism and gout. She slipped in and out of consciousness. On January 5, 1589, she was conscious long enough to dictate her will and to make a confession before taking communion. She died later that afternoon. Henry and some members of her court were at her bedside.

Catherine's body was embalmed and lay in state. In the

These naked effigies of Catherine de' Medici and Henry II now mark their tombs at the royal chapel of Saint-Denis.

streets of Paris, crowds waved torches and celebrated her death. Huguenots lit bonfires as they paraded to celebrate the judgment of God against the wicked.

Tradition dictated that Catherine would be buried at Saint-Denis, the burial place of France's kings and queens. But an accident in the embalming process required a hurried burial in an unmarked grave. The body stayed there for twenty-one years until a member of the court had it moved to Saint-Denis. When the building there was demolished in 1719, the corpse was moved into the abbey. In 1793, a revolutionary mob would dig it up and toss it into a mass grave.

Henry III seemed too stunned by his mother's death to do anything useful. He spent hours shut up in his rooms writing justifications for all his actions. When Henry of Navarre offered a cease-fire, the king agreed. Their representatives signed an agreement on April 2, 1589.

The end of hostilities, which Catherine had worked so long and hard for, seemed to be close. Although the Catholic League and the Vatican rose up to protest the agreement, Henry III agreed to travel to meet Navarre in a castle near the city of Tours. In an emotional meeting, Navarre knelt before his brother-in-law and proclaimed his obedience. Both men declared their support for the other.

They joined their forces and headed back to Paris. The assassination of the Duke of Guise had left the Catholic League without a strong leader. Catherine's death had probably removed another obstacle to peace. In Paris, the Catholic League was growing desperate as they received word that all the villages and towns the combined kings passed through were greeting them warmly. Clearly, the people of France were weary of war; most would accept religious toleration if it would end the bloodshed.

But France's misery was not yet over. Less than five weeks later, Henry and Navarre set up camp on the outskirts of Paris. The plan was to attack, but Henry wanted to give the Catholic League a chance to surrender. Then, early on the morning of August 1, a monk approached King Henry III. He claimed to be carrying an urgent letter. As Henry began to read the letter, the monk pulled out a knife and stabbed him in the side. The thirty-eight-year-old king lingered through the night but died the next morning. The Valois family was no more. Before dying, Henry named Navarre as his heir. He was now Henry IV of France, the first of the Bourbon kings. He would rule until 1789.

Meanwhile, in Paris, the Catholic League refused to

accept a Protestant king. They named the old cardinal of Bourbon the king. Philip II of Spain also made a claim to the throne, based upon the daughter he had with Elizabeth, Catherine's oldest child. He appealed to the pope for support.

It took five years for Henry IV to reconsolidate France beneath his control. He was able to take advantage of divisions within the Catholic League, and between the League and the Vatican. When it became apparent that the only thing standing between him and the throne, and peace, was conversion, Henry converted to Catholicism in 1593. Legend has it that he was heard to mutter "Paris is worth a mass," before accepting communion.

In 1598, Henry IV issued the Edict of Nantes, which called for a measure of religious toleration. This time the exhausted county accepted an end to the religious wars. Henry then turned his attention to reforming the governmental administration, rebuilding the army, and instituting financial reforms. He became a much beloved and respected king. Nevertheless, he was assassinated by a Protestant fanatic on May 14, 1610.

The religious wars that divided France finally abated, only to be supplanted by conflicts arising from the continued social and economic disparity. Nearly two hundred years later, France would again erupt into tumult—this time, the king and queen would lose their heads and the monarchy would be (temporarily) abolished. The united France that Catherine de' Medici dreamed of did become a reality, but only after exacting a terrible toll in blood.

Timeline

1519 Caterina Maria Romola de' Medici is born in Florence, Italy.

1533 Marries at Marseilles, France.

1544 Son Francis is born.

1545 Daughter Elizabeth is born.

1547 Husband assumes throne as Henry II.

1547 Daughter Claude is born.

1549 Son Louis is born.

1550 Son Charles is born.

1551 Son Edouard (reanamed Henry in 1564; became the Duke of Anjou in 1566) is born.

1553 Daughter Marguerite (Margo) is born.

1555 Son Hercule (later the Duke of Alençon) is born.

1559 Henry II dies; Francis becomes King Francis II.

1560 Francis dies; Charles becomes King Charles IX; Catherine becomes regent.

1572 Massacre of St. Bartholomew's Day.

1574 Charles IX dies.

1575 Henry, Duke of Anjou becomes King Henry III.

1588 Day of the Barricades.

1589 Catherine dies, probably of pleurisy, on January 5.

TIMELINE - FRANCE

58-51 B.C.E.   Julius Caesar conquers Gaul.

987	Hugh Capet is crowned king.
1337-1453	France defeats England in Hundred Years War.
1643-1715	Louis XIV rules France and consolidates absolute authority of the French king.
1789-1799	French Revolution takes place, ends absolute rule by kings.
1804	Napoleon founds First Empire.
1848	Revolutionists establish Second Republic.
1870-1871	Third Republic is begun.
1914-1918	Fights for Allies in World War I.
1939-1940	Fights for Allies in World War II.
1940	Is defeated by Germany.
1946	Establishes the Fourth Republic.
1949	Joins the North Atlantic Treaty Organization.
1957	Joins the European Economic Community.
1958	Adopts new constitution under President de Gaulle.
1998	Is fourth largest contributor to United Nations.
1999	Accepts introduction of the *euro* , EEC monetary standard.

Sources

CHAPTER ONE: Born into Chaos

p. 21, "refused with wonderful firmness . . ." Hugh Ross Williamson, *Catherine de' Medici* (New York: The Viking Press, 1973), 24.

p. 22, "Will they dare . . ." Ibid.

CHAPTER TWO: The Valois Court

p. 25, "dissatisfies the entire nation" Williamson, *Catherine de' Medici*, 39.

p. 28, "He laughs or makes any sign." Irene Mahoney, *Madame Catherine* (New York: Coward, McCann & Geoghegan, Inc., 1975), 29.

p. 35, "[Catherine] possesses extraordinary . . ." Mark Strage, *Women of Power: The Life and Times of Catherine de' Medici* (New York: Harcourt Brace Jovanovich, 1976), 84.

CHAPTER THREE: Queen of France

p. 46, "I am going to be . . ." Strage, *Women of Power*, 39.

p. 46, "who wishes to maintain . . ." Niccolò Machiavelli, *The Prince and The Discourses* (New York: The Modern Library, 1950), 73.

p. 46, "it is better to be impetuous . . ." Ibid., 94.

p. 48, "she is so much loved . . ." Mahoney, *Madame Catherine*, 44.

p. 50, "you [Henry] have given away . . ." Strage, *Women of Power*, 95.

p. 52, "in such a feeble . . . " Mahoney, *Madame Catherine*, 56.

p. 52, "Conforming myself . . ." Ibid.

CHAPTER FOUR: So Much Blood

p. 60, "My sweet God . . ." Strage, *Women of Power,* 123.

p. 65, "God has taken him . . ." Mahoney, *Madame Catherine,* 74.

p. 67, "Thanks be to God. . . ." Ibid., 81.

p. 67, "There is no one. . . ." Ibid., 82.

p. 70, "I do not believe . . ." Williamson, *Catherine de' Medici,* 118

CHAPTER FIVE: Queen Mother

p. 72, "To consent that a widow . . ." Mahoney, *Madame Catherine,* 77.

p. 73, "help [him] govern the state . . ." Ibid., 75.

p. 73, "Force and violence pertain . . ." R.J. Knecht, *Catherine de' Medici* (London: Longman, 1998), 69.

p. 77, "I see so much . . ." Ibid., 88.

p. 77, "I do not see any great hope . . ." Mahoney, *Madame Catherine,* 93.

p. 77, "maintain the honor of God . . ." Ibid.

p. 77, "Since you rely on . . ." Knecht, *Catherine de' Medici,* 89.

p. 79, "My courage is as great . . ." Ibid., 90.

p. 79, "Normandy was so harassed . . ." Mahoney, *Madame Catherine,* 98.

p. 79, "one of the greatest . . . play the captain." Strage, *Women of Power,* 129.

p. 85, "I now live . . ." Ibid., 137.

p. 87, "God will not permit this...." Mahoney, *Madame Catherine,* 127.

CHAPTER SIX: Planning a Wedding

p. 89, "There are circumstances..." Knecht, *Catherine de' Medici,* 121.

p. 89, "I have to carry . . ." Ibid., 125.

p. 90, "Louis XIII by the grace of God . . ." Mahoney, *Madame Catherine*, 123.

p. 90, "The man has gone mad . . ." Ibid.

p. 100, "I blazed in diamonds . . ." Strage, *Women of Power*, 153.

p. 101, "constrained to work..." Ibid., 188.

p. 103, "Am I never to be..." Ibid., 189.

p. 104, "Kill the admiral..." Williamson, *Catherine de' Medici*, 218.

CHAPTER SEVEN: Kill Them Aall

p. 109, "One [a leader] must color . . ." Will Durant, *The Story of Civilization: Part VI, The Reformation* (New York: Simon and Schuster, 1957), 563.

p. 110, "I hardly know how . . ." Mahoney, *Madame Catherine*, 181.

p. 112, "The King is reduced . . ." Ibid., 194.

p. 113, "The King is dead . . . Henry III" Ibid., 202.

CHAPTER EIGHT: No Peace

p. 115, "I am sure that . . ." Knecht, *Catherine de' Medici*, 173.

p. 118, "We have decided to win . . ." Ibid., 184.

p. 118, "I will go myself..." Williamson, *Catherine de' Medici*, 253.

p. 122, "disapproves of everything . . ." Knecht, *Catherine de' Medici*, 189.

p. 122, "I beg you to control...." Mahoney, *Madame Catherine*, 235.

p. 125, "Come to dine or . . ." Ibid., 240.

CHAPTER NINE: A Race for the Throne

p. 128, "I cannot believe..." Mahoney, *Madame Catherine*, 256.

p. 133, "Believe me, I am going to . . . ." Ibid., 278.

p. 135, "for the conservation of the Catholic religion . . ." Ibid., 240.

p. 136, "One can hardly get the king . . ." Ibid., 298.

p. 136, "Had a sword . . ." Ibid.

p. 137, "I realize that God has given. . . ." Ibid., 296.

CHAPTER TEN: Choosing a New King

p. 138, "God must be very angry . . ." Mahoney, *Madame Catherine*, 302.

p 139, "Long live the Duke of Guise!" Ibid., 314.

p. 145, "Oh, wretched man!…" Knecht, *Catherine de' Medici*, 267.

p. 145, "You will be . . ." Mahoney, *Madame Catherine*, 333.

p. 148, "Paris is worth . . ." Williamson, *Catherine de' Medici*, 281.

Bibliography

Baumgartner, Frederic. J. *France in the Sixteenth Century*. New York: St. Martin's Press, 1995.

De Castries, Duc. *The Lives of the Kings and Queens of France*. New York: Alfred A.Knopf, 1979.

Durant, Will. *The Story of Civilization: Part V. The Renaissance*. New York: Simon and Schuster, 1953.

———. *The Story of Civilization: Part VI, The Reformation*. New York: Simon and Schuster, 1957.

Green, V. H. H. *Renaissance and Reformation*. London, Edward Arnold & Co., 1952.

Knecht, R.J., *Catherine de' Medici*. London: Longman, 1998.

Machiavelli, Niccolò. *The Prince and The Discourses*, New York: The Modern Library, 1950.

Mahoney, Irene. *Madame Catherine*. New York: Coward, McCann. & Geoghegan, Inc., 1975.

Maurois, André. *A History of France*. New York: Farrar, Straus and Cudahy, 1956.

Neale, J.E. *The Age of Catherine de' Medici*. London: Jonathan Cape, 1943.

Romier, Lucien. *A History of France*. Translated and completed by A L. Rowse. New York: St. Martin's Press, 1953.

Strage, Mark. *Women of Power: The Life and Times of Catherine de' Medici*. New York: Harcourt Brace Jovanovich, 1976.

Williamson, Hugh Ross. *Catherine de' Medici*. New York: The Viking Press, 1973.

Web sites

http://www.kings.edu/womens_history/cathymedici.html
A biography of Catherine de' Medici from King's College.

http://www.historylearningsite.co.uk/FWR.htm
A thoughtful and comprehensive description of the Wars of Religion and their causes, including a timeline and an article about Catherine de' Medici's importance.

http://www.beyond.fr/history/religion.html
A quick overview of the main players and events in the Wars of Religion.

Index